THIS BOOK is published with the aid of the **Bookmarks Publishing Co-operative**. Many socialists have a few savings put aside, probably in a bank or savings bank. While it's there, this money is being re-loaned by the bank to some business or other to further the aims of capitalism. We believe it is better loaned to a socialist venture to further the struggle for socialism. That's how the co-operative works: in return for a loan, repayable at a month's notice, members receive free copies of books published by Bookmarks, plus other advantages. The co-operative has about 130 members at the time this book is published, from as far apart as London and Australia, Canada and Norway.

Like to know more? Write to the **Bookmarks Publishing Co-operative**, 265 Seven Sisters Road, London N4 2DE, England.

BRITAIN ON
THE BRINK OF
REVOLUTION

1919

CHANIE ROSENBERG

Bookmarks
London, Chicago and Melbourne

1919: BRITAIN ON THE BRINK OF REVOLUTION
by Chanie Rosenberg

Published January 1987
Bookmarks, 265 Seven Sisters Road, London N4 2DE, England.
Bookmarks, PO Box 16085, Chicago, IL 60616, USA.
Bookmarks, GPO Box 1473N, Melbourne 3001, Australia.

ISBN 0 906224 34 9

Printed by Cox and Wyman Limited, Reading, England.
Typeset by Kate Macpherson, Clevedon, Avon.
Design by Roger Huddle.

BOOKMARKS is linked to an international grouping of socialist organisations:

AUSTRALIA: **International Socialists**, GPO Box 1473N, Melbourne 3001.
BELGIUM: **Socialisme International**, 9 rue Marexhe, 4400 Herstal, Liege.
BRITAIN: **Socialist Workers Party**, PO Box 82, London E3.
CANADA: **International Socialists**, PO Box 339, Station E, Toronto, Ontario.
DENMARK: **Internationale Socialister**, Morten Borupsgade 18, kld, 8000
    Arhus C.
FRANCE: **Socialisme International** (correspondence to Yves Coleman, BP 407,
    Paris Cedex 05).
IRELAND: **Socialist Workers Movement**, PO Box 1648, Dublin 8.
NORWAY: **Internasjonale Sosialister**, Postboks 5370, Majorstua, 0304 Oslo 3.
UNITED STATES: **International Socialist Organization**, PO Box 16085, Chicago,
    Illinois 60616.
WEST GERMANY: **Sozialistische Arbeiter Gruppe**, Wolfgangstrasse 81,
    D–6000 Frankfurt 1.

Contents

Acknowledgements

I wish to acknowledge the assistance of Tony Cliff, Geoff Ellen, Donny Gluckstein, Alastair Hatchett and Pete Marsden, for supplying useful material, making helpful comments and smoothing over rough patches. The librarians at the Public Records Office, London School of Economics and Colindale Newspaper Library deserve thanks for helpful and patient assistance.
Chanie Rosenberg

Chanie Rosenberg is a member of the Socialist Workers Party. Among her previous publications are **Education and Society** (1974) and **Education and Revolution** (1975).

INTRODUCTION

'IT CAN'T HAPPEN HERE' is an oft-repeated cry. In fact it nearly did. In 1919 Britain came closer to a workers' revolution than ever before or since.

The Russian revolution of 1917 lit a flame which flared all over Europe. There were revolutions in Germany, Austria, Hungary, and the growth of mass Communist Parties in Italy, France, Czechoslovakia and elsewhere. Britain in 1919 was part of this rising revolutionary wave. As the First World War came to its bitter end, there was turmoil in all classes of society. Past conditions could no longer be tolerated. To counter discontent prime minister Lloyd George promised 'a land fit for heroes', and in the closing days of 1918 won a landslide election on the strength of this.

But that dream evaporated fast with the dawn of 1919. The workers continued to suffer all the privations of the war period — shortages of food, housing and other things, now aggravated by rapid price rises, unemployment, snail's-pace demobilisation of men from the forces and, to add insult to injury, the conspicuous luxury enjoyed by the war profiteers. The workers rebelled in a massive wave of strikes, with working days lost leaping from nearly six million in 1918 to nearly 35 million in 1919 — which was an average of more than 100,000 workers on strike every working day.

The target of the workers' discontent was the state. The reason was obvious. For the efficient prosecution of the war the state had become the overall controller of all the major industries. It thus became the natural focus for protest. It faced a serious crisis from another quarter too. The state reeled under the impact of mutiny by its own soldiers, sailors and airmen at home and abroad. Late in 1918 there was a widespread strike of police, whose discontent seethed throughout most of 1919.

The ruling class governs by force and persuasion, stick and carrot, the balance between them changing according to circumstances. In Franco's Spain or Chile in 1973 the working class was crushed by brute force. In the bourgeois democracies of the Western world, however, persuasion takes precedence.

In Lloyd George's Cabinet (which was still called the War Cabinet) Winston Churchill, minister of munitions, later secretary of state for war, was in favour of using the big stick. Lloyd George wanted to achieve the same result: the smashing of workers' resistance, but he believed it was necessary to concede enough to defuse a dangerous situation, postpone the day of reckoning, and then, when the revolutionary fervour had sufficiently abated, plunge the knife in for the kill.

But the government has no direct communication with the workers. To control them it needs the mediation of a go-between, whose interests, at least in part, coincide with its own. These are the trade union officials. They had to head the workers' movement in order to behead it. And for this the government had to pay, however much that hurt. As William Brace, a miners' leader and member of parliament, explained when the prime minister was trying to put off an imminent miners' strike, 'unless we can go [to the miners' conference] with an overwhelming case for delay, then we shall stand discredited before our people, and a discredited body of leaders is of no value to the men they lead and of no value to the country of whom they form a part and whom they would like to serve.'[1]

That the Cabinet did not split wide open behind Lloyd George and Chuchill is because the workers failed to force the issue to that extreme. In the absence of any alternative leadership to that of the trade union and Labour Party leaders, to which the workers could turn to carry their fight forward, Lloyd George's tactics of using both carrot and stick worked like a dream.

It is not the case that Lloyd George was sure he would master the situation. The Cabinet often did not know whether they were

8

coming or going. Lloyd George went on assuming, or pretending, that there was a revolutionary crisis long after that danger was over and his devious tactic was no longer needed. When it was clear that the revolutionary wave had passed, he was kicked out of the government.

The crisis had many focal points — the army, police, engineers, but above all the great industrial unions of miners, railwaymen and transport workers, forged together in the Triple Alliance. We shall trace their struggles in turn, look at the various ways the government handled them, show the key role of the trade union officials, and finally examine the outcome.

I

THE BACKGROUND to the 1919 crisis was the First World War of 1914-18. In November 1917 the soldiers and sailors of Russia joined with the workers and peasants to make a revolution that put an end to the war on the Eastern Front. On the Western Front the British government did not expect the war to end in 1918, but decided to 'fix the culminating period for our supreme military effort on the Western Front not later than 1st July, 1919.'[1] But in November 1918 the soldiers and sailors of Germany too joined with the workers to make a revolution that put an end to the war altogether.

Revolution, then, was the spectre that haunted Lloyd George's newly-formed Cabinet. Unit after unit of the British army, navy and air force mutinied in January and February 1919, against the background of a rapidly rising strike wave in industry.

Churchill, as minister for munitions, was demanding huge forces for the war against Bolshevism in Russia. He wanted existing troops to be retained and more conscripted. The men said No! The universal cry was: 'The war is over. We won't fight in Russia. We mean to go home.' And they mutinied to get there.

The revolts displayed varying degrees of organisation, ranging from elementary outbursts to highly-organised strikes with soldiers' committees made up of other ranks (and occasionally including officers) which both represented the soldiers to higher authority and organised the protests in the camps and on the demonstrations. Demobilisation was the universal issue, but once the movement started it drew like a magnet all the multitude of grievances suffered by the troops at the end of the four years of slaughter.

The very first mutiny gives an idea of their character. It occurred in Folkestone on Friday 3 January 1919, when 2,000 soldiers were ordered to embark for service abroad. They refused, gathered others behind them, and marched 10,000-strong to the town hall where they held a meeting. The boats sailed empty, and assurances were given of speedy demobilisation and *voluntary* embarcation to France. But next day new orders for the embarcation of 'a certain number' provoked another demonstration, this time to picket the harbour and the incoming troop-trains of men returning from leave; all joined the strike. They tore down a notice 'For Officers Only' above the door of a comfortable waiting room, formed a 'Soldiers' Union' and elected a committee of nine to represent them at a meeting with the general and town commandant. The composition of the committee was entirely rank and file: a sergeant, a corporal, a gunner, the rest privates (several of whom were trade unionists). To make sure they were properly represented, the 10,000 marched to the meeting place to await the result. That day the ships sailed for France with officers only.

The government handled the situation with kid gloves. It delayed no longer, and formalities for demobilisation were completed in all the camps affected that very night by staff hastily sent from London.[2]

News of this strike reached the newspapers, but censorship immediately clamped down on reports of all subsequent mutinies. This damped down but by no means extinguished the fire.

Over the next fortnight there followed nearly fifty other mutinies, involving tens of thousands of troops all over Britain and abroad. These are colourfully described in Andrew Rothstein's book, **The Soldiers' Strikes of 1919**. All demanded speedier demobilisation and no fighting in Russia, but other grievances piled up.

Food was bad. For example in Uxbridge, 'the food had been rotten since the Armistice, one loaf between eight men, five days a week sausage'. The men upset the tables, then formed a Messing

Committee, a Grievance Committee, and sent a deputation to the War Office.[3]

So were the sanitary conditions. For example, at Biggin Hill there were 'indescribable sanitary conditions, with eight washbasins for 700 men.'[4] Other frequent grievances were unnecessary guard duties, drill, fatigues, too much red tape, having to do civilian work at rotten pay. And demands included the abolition of Sunday church parades, the stopping of exploitation by officers who required the men to do private jobs for them, no swearing when orders were given, 'to be treated as men, not as children by the officers', no victimisation.[5]

Some mutinies were carried right to the door of the Cabinet. On 8 January the Army Service Corps of 4,000 men at Park Royal in North West London elected a committee to demand: (1) speedier demobilisation; (2) reveille to be sounded at 6.30 in the morning, not 5.30; (3) work to finish at 4.30 in the afternoon, not 5.30; (4) no men over 41 to be sent overseas; (5) all training to stop; (6) a large reduction of guard and picket duty; (7) no compulsory church parade; (8) no drafts for Russia; (9) a committee of one NCO (non-commissioned officer) and two privates to control messing arrangements for each company; (10) a written guarantee of no victimisation.

Despite the commanding officer's agreeing to most of these, 1,500 men next day went to Whitehall to present their demands themselves to the prime minister. They defied General Feilding, commander of the London District, who tried to stop them at Paddington and again at the Horse Guards Parade ground, and marched to Downing Street, encouraged by crowds of bystanders.

Inside Number 10 the Cabinet were very jittery. Lloyd George proclaimed himself ready to meet the soldiers. Lord Milner, the secretary for war, feared this would be a bad precedent, as 'similar processions would march on London from all over the country.' The Chief of the Imperial General Staff said 'the Prime Minister should not confer with soldiers' delegates who had disregarded their Officers. The soldiers' delegation bore a dangerous resemblance to a *Soviet*. If such a practice were to spread the consequences would be disastrous.' Sir Eric Geddes, minister of reconstruction, suggested 'the men might be drawn up in the Horse Guards Parade in military formation under their officers'; but General Sir William Robertson, the General Officer Commanding Home Forces, explained that 'the officers were not with the men'.[6]

General Robertson was sent out to the soldiers and agreed to meet a deputation of one corporal, one lance-corporal and one private for half an hour. The men meanwhile refused an officers' invitation for them to go back to camp, insisting on waiting for the return of their deputation. Their demands being acceded to, they returned, held a meeting and expressed their satisfaction.[7]

At Milford Haven men on the patrol vessel *HMS Kilbride* mutinied, refusing to do two watches for the pay they were receiving. They asked to see the captain, but this was refused; in reply, they refused to go to sea. The captain went ashore to report the matter, whereupon they hauled down the naval flag and hoisted the Red Flag.[8] The **Herald**, edited by George Lansbury, in an editorial on 11 January, aptly questioned: 'Have you wondered why demobilisation is so slow? Perhaps you think it is merely "red tape". It is not. It is the Red Flag — in Russia.'[9] The article continued: 'Our masters . . . are trembling for more than their *Russian* dividends; they are trembling for the security of the dividend-hunting system all the world over.'[10]

One of the most highly organised mutinies took place in Calais and the surrounding area. It was precipitated by the arrest on 2 January of a soldier prominent in the agitation over demobilisation, and culminated in a strike lasting from 27-31 January. Other issues — bad food and pay, overwork, and so on — fanned the discontent. Women nurses put forward demands. Some of the soldiers demanded permission to attend a 'Hands Off Russia' demonstration called by the British Socialist Party to be held at the Albert Hall in London on 8 February.

Parties of men were sent to all camps in the Calais area and found them all solid; about 20,000 men in all were out. There were strike committees functioning in all the camps, with a headquarters at Valdelièvre, which issued daily 'orders' and even permits. A soldiers' council was elected, called 'The Calais Area Soldiers' and Sailors' Association', with four or more delegates from the larger camps and two each from the smaller. It met in cafes, 20-30 servicemen regularly attending.

Reinforcements were rushed to quell the riot, but 'the officer commanding the leave camp was ejected by the men during the morning'. The general who then took over posted infantry and machine guns at the camp, but fraternisation between the mutineers and those set to guard them frustrated his efforts.

At that the authorities gave in.[11]

The Defence of the Realm Act (DORA) was still in force and mutiny subject to the death penalty. But when the commander-in-chief, General Haig, wanted to shoot the leaders of the Calais strike, even Churchill had to demur — for fear of repercussions at home.[12] One revolt only appears to have drawn punishment, and that was not in the army but the navy, where men were on long-term engagements — the Milford Haven 'Red Flag' incident, where one sailor was sentenced to two years' hard labour, three to one year and three to 90 days detention. For the rest it was concessions all round and denunciations avoided. In at least one case there was even appreciation of the orderly behaviour of the troops.

The British soldiers and sailors were as mutinous abroad as at home. In the Western battle zone troops threatened 'they would demobilise themselves if the government didn't'. In Salonika a whole company of men 'were disgracefully abusive to their officers'. In Archangel in north Russia the 13th battalion of the Yorkshire Light Infantry — sent to fight against the Revolution — revolted and set up a *soviet*, or soldiers' council, according to one authority. Field Marshal Lord Ironside admitted 'that we are drawing terribly near to the end of our tether as an efficient fighting force . . .' After the meeting of the 13th Yorkshires, the British authorities had arranged to turn the machine guns of the White Russians against the British battalion 'in the event of an open mutiny'.[13]

Soldiers abroad suffered harsher penalties, as without civilian support it was easier to use force, but still no blood was shed.

The reliability of the state's forces of repression became a factor of key importance, as on the industrial front there was a rash of strikes, and key sectors of the working class — the miners and railwaymen — were threatening to come out. It was a situation that threatened the government's very existence. Towards the end of January, to try to keep control of the situation, Churchill issued a circular to all army commanders requiring them to report weekly on the following questions:

'Secret and urgent . . .

(1)　(a) Will troops in various areas respond to orders for assistance to preserve the public peace?

(b) Will they assist in strike breaking?

(c) Will they parade for draft to overseas, especially in Russia?

(d) . . . Do they consider the policy of dividing the Army into the classes demobilisables and non-demobilisables, a sound one, and, if so, do they think that the line of cleavage has been equitably fixed? Is there any dissatisfaction with either the principles or the details . . . and, if so, what are your recommendations?

(e) Any other information or suggestions.

(2)　You will please give your own views for the information of the General Officer Commanding.

(3)　You will, of course, understand that any material change in a situation, and any cases of disorder or indiscipline are to be reported at once.

(4)　The above is to be circulated to all officers commanding Stations, Formations, and Units in the area under your command and to save time you will please instruct Officers Commanding Stations to forward reports under the headings given above direct to these Headquarters attaching any report from an Officer Commanding Formation or Unit which is of importance. They will quote the above number and mark the reports 'Secret and urgent'.

(5)　I am to add that the above is required with a view to the establishment of an efficient intelligence service whereby the Army Council can keep its finger on the pulse of the troops, and that the information desired is required for the information of the Secretary of State.'

The following was also issued to Station Commanders:

'Will you please let me have the following information . . . as speedily as possible with regard to the Units on the Station under your command:

(a) Whether there is any growth of trade unionism among them.

(b) The effect outside trade unions have on them.

(c) Whether any agitation from internal or external sources is affecting them.

(d) Whether any soldiers' councils have been formed.

(e) Whether any demobilisation troubles are occurring and if so (i) what troops are demonstrating; (ii) the numbers involved; (iii) what their grievances are; (iv) what has been done.'[14]

The existence of this circular caused a storm of protest when it was sensationally exposed by the **Daily Herald** on 13 May 1919, and fuelled a clamour for direct action against the war in Russia.

Prior to this the Cabinet had been receiving alarmist — and unfortunately exaggerated — reports from its agents, such as this report of 10 January to Bonar Law, the deputy prime minister:

. . . a certain section of the workers (whose names and activities are well known to Scotland Yard and the Home Office) are only too ready and eager to fan and foment a passing grievance to inveigle the soldiers into an alliance with themselves, on the lines of the Soviet Committees. The ultimate end of this manoeuvre would be Revolution and a Soviet form of Government.

The dangers consequent upon even the slightest success of such a scheme must be patent to anyone who has studied the course of events in Russia. The spread of this spirit is alarming, and evidence can be obtained of a determined effort to emulate the Russian Bolshevik movement of this country.[15]

Churchill's Circular was designed to thwart this unity of purpose between workers and soldiers. Unity of purpose was to be a government monopoly. The War Office spokesman in the House of Commons the day after its publication, showed the government's generalised approach.

16

Captain Guest (for the Secretary of State for War) said that the document . . . was a confidential circular issued some three months ago, for which the War Office accept sole responsibility, at a time when the country was threatened with a strike which would have brought the vital services, including food supplies, of the nation to a standstill . . . The Govt . . . conceived it to be their duty to the country to take steps to prevent such a state of affairs arising. Information for this and other purposes . . . was needed and the method adopted was by no means improper under the peculiar circumstances then prevailing . . . it was clearly necessary that the Government should be informed of the sentiments of the troops before framing such a policy as would safeguard the public interests.[16]

The soldiers' strikes achieved a number of things.

First, the march of the privates and NCOs on to the stage of history terrified the Cabinet, because it saw its means of strike-breaking and repression of industrial unrest evaporating before its very eyes. A Cabinet memorandum, criticising Churchill's demand to slow down demobilisation and step up compulsory recruitment particularly for the Russian front, gives the reasoning behind the soft approach to the soldiers. C Addison, president of the Local Government Board, says:

I am strongly of opinion that the suggestion to renew recruiting under the Military Service Acts is open to the gravest objection . . . The present time, when industrial unrest prevails to acutely, would be a most unfortunate time at which to throw into the arena new causes of distrust and trouble, which would certainly be represented by not a few Labour leaders as adopted partly because of industrial troubles.[17]

The arguments went on from meeting to meeting, with the generals and Churchill doing their best to feed the flames — but with a growing opposition led by the prime minister.[18] On 14 January Haig and other generals claimed that 'the state of the army is deplorable', on the 15th that the army was 'rapidly disappearing', on the 16th Churchill wrote that 'the army is liquefying fast', and on the 17th Sir Henry Wilson, Chief of the Imperial General Staff, told Churchill: 'We are sitting on the top of a mine which may go up at any minute.'

Even the warmongering Churchill was forced to write to Lloyd George on the 18th about discontent in the British army in France, and to cable him on the 19th that if there were any further delay in demobilisation, there would be nothing left of the army but a 'demoralised and angry mob.' By the 22nd Wilson was saying: 'We dare not give an unpopular order to the troops and discipline is a thing of the past.' Haig said that if the existing state of things continued, by the end of February he would have no army left in France. Bonar Law was 'terrified'.[19]

On the same day Lord Curzon, acting secretary of state for foreign affairs, said that he was alarmed by the fact that no concerted action was being taken by the various departments 'with regard to combating the spread of Bolshevism in this country', and suggested a minister without portfolio be placed in charge of co-ordinating activities of different departments in this direction.[20]

On 27 January Churchill wrote to Lloyd George pressing for reinforcement of the Russian intervention until victory was obtained. At the same time he was forced to admit that 'unfortunately we have not the power — our orders would not be obeyed, I regret to say.'[21] On 10 February Churchill said that British enterprises in all directions in Russia were crumbling.[22]

There was complete disheartenment on all sides and normal punitive military rules and procedures had to be scrapped for the time being in favour of the 'softly, softly' approach.

The second result of the soldiers' strikes was that Churchill did not get his fighting reinforcements in Russia, Lloyd George agreeing only to some auxiliaries going 'to secure the health, comfort and nourishment of the troops there.'[23] He reasoned that 'if demobilisation had been stopped in order to divert the troops from France to Odessa or Archangel there would have been a mutiny. The attempt to raise a force of volunteers for the purpose of waging war against the Bolsheviks was a miserable failure.'[24]

It is interesting to note that Lenin wrote on 21 January 1919:

'Attempts to conquer Russia, which require a long-term occupation army of a million men, are the most certain road to the most rapid extension of proletarian revolution to the Entente countries.'[25]

The third result was a rapid acceleration of demobilisation. Of the six million in the army at the end of the war, only 261,000 had been demobbed by the end of 1918 — an average 37,000 a week. As a result of the speeding up which began in the second week of January, the numbers increased dramatically, and by the end of the month nearly one million had been demobbed. By the end of February the figure was 1,713,000, and the discharge continued steadily till four million had been released by mid-December 1919.[26] On 28 January the Cabinet also awarded the armed forces a pay increase, 'frankly to allay unrest.'[27]

The Cabinet continued to be jittery about the use of troops in strike situations and never moved on this front without questioning the War Office on their reliability. In a discussion on 30 January on whether to use troops against the Glasgow 'Forty Hours' strike, 'it was pointed out that, during one of the big railway strikes in peace time, a few soldiers had been employed as engine drivers and guards. General Childs said that this was true; a few men had been so employed, but at that time we had a well-disciplined and ignorant army, whereas now we had an army educated and ill-disciplined.'[28]

For a threatened electricity strike on 6 February the Admiralty was asked to supply electrical mechanics as blacklegs. On 5 February the First Lord of the Admiralty had reported to the War Cabinet that 'it would be very undesirable to make use of them as they had been badly reported upon and might refuse to obey orders.' But if they were used, to make sure no fraternisation took place, the Admiralty 'would undertake that no group of men would be put into any power station, except under an officer, and it must be understood that these men were not to associate with anyone else.'[29] In the event the electricity strike did not materialise.

Even the small but superior air force was contaminated. Over the issue of the same electrical strike, Churchill remarked:

with regard to the suggestion to use skilled men from the air force, that they were the least disciplined and most tradeunionised of His Majesty's Forces. They . . . were hardly distinguishable from trade unionists . . . He deprecated their use in industrial disputes, except in the last resort.

Austin Chamberlain, chancellor of the exchequer, noted that:

we were proposing to count on the skilled artisans in the army. We could not be certain of them. They might come in, and they might not . . . On the next day — if they failed us — we might ask them to quell a riot, and having refused before, they might refuse again.[30]

What was the consciousness of these workers in uniform?

History works in mysterious ways. In a time of deep social unrest, even the Tory press may act as a stimulant to revolution. By far the most widely-read newspapers in the barracks and camps at the end of the war were the **Daily Mail** and **Daily Express**, both Tory in outlook but pandering to the massive desire for demobilisation among the soldiers. In a Cabinet memorandum, headed 'Fortnightly Report on Revolutionary Organisations in the United Kingdom and Morale Abroad', and dated 13 January 1919, Basil Home Thomson of the Special Branch, later director of the government's intelligence service, points to the demoralising influence of these two papers:

The trouble may be largely ascribed to the action of a few newspapers. My correspondents abroad have been pointing out for some time the bad effect on the troops of the Paris edition of **The Daily Mail**, with its Labour column and its articles on Demobilisation. Unfortunately, it has been practically the only paper accessible to the troops day by day.[31]

The **Daily Mail** ranted against the 'mass of red tape and official forms' cluttering the demobilisation process (5 December 1918) and exclaimed, 'there is a stoppage in the pipe somewhere . . . The machine must be speeded up' (11 December 1918). A **Daily Express** editorial was headed 'Withdraw the Troops from Russia' (4 January 1919).[32]

Another big influence to which soldiers turned was the demagogue adventurer Horatio Bottomley. His weekly journal **John**

Bull combined jingoism with scandal about the war profiteers and corruption among officials, with stories of ill-treatment of soldiers' relatives, and denunciations of strikes and socialism. All Britain was covered with his posters 'Write to **John Bull** about it', and tens of thousands did.[33]

The left Labour paper, George Lansbury's **Herald**, which was a spirited socialist agitator on behalf of the soldiers, had only a tiny influence compared to those mentioned, partly because the authorities sabotaged its circulation to the troops.

The Labour Party at the time was a pro-war, patriotic, chauvinist party. The revolutionary left was small and fragmented. The largest party, the British Socialist Party (BSP), was a propaganda organisation which believed that agitation for strikes would be 'an impertinent interference in a field with which they had nothing to do.'[34] The leaders of the Socialist Labour Party (SLP) led mass strikes but kept politics out of them in a separate compartment. The Independent Labour Party (ILP) was a 'centrist' organisation uninvolved in industrial struggle; during the war they had been pacifists, imprisoned as conscientious objectors by the hundreds, and so useless as soldier-agitators. Such parties could not grow and aim to influence the soldiers' movement.

By themselves the soldiers' strikes could achieve only what they did achieve — a speed-up of demobilisation. Soldiers, not being at the point of production, are not *part* of the working class, even though they come *from* the working class, whose sufferings and feelings they share and to which they will return. Hence the participation of soldiers in an effort to smash the state machine can be developed only if their strike movement is brought under the leadership of the working class, ultimately organised in workers' and soldiers' councils.

This potential existed in 1919. The party to develop it did not. The foundations for such a party were laid by the uniting of revolutionary socialist elements from the BSP, some from the ILP, and later the SLP, to form the Communist Party. But that was during 1920-21, after the revolutionary opportunity had slipped by.

Events in Russia showed the possibilities. There the Bolsheviks worked actively among the Russian troops, taking the lead wherever possible not only in agitation against the officers and army hierarchy, but also in propaganda against the war and the capitalist system of which the war was a product. In the factories at home too, the Bolsheviks were agitating against the war and the capitalist system. As the struggle developed, with the revolutionary peasantry also fighting against the landlords, the three strands united in the Soviets of Workers, Soldiers and Peasants. At the time of the February revolution of 1917 the Bolsheviks were a small party of 2,000 in Petrograd, 23,600 in the whole country. Their lead in the fight for 'Bread, Land and Peace' — encapsulating the demands of workers, peasants and soldiers — drew the revolutionary masses behind them until they became a majority of the working class and could take power in November 1917.

It would be wrong to make a close analogy between events in Russia and Britain. The Russian army was defeated, the British victorious; the slaughter, huge as it was for British troops, was much greater for the Russians, the cut in the standard of living more extreme, and the resulting anti-war movement much bigger. But, *mutatis mutandis*, in Britain the elements of explosive strike action and mutinous troops and police existed side by side, and could have been developed, even if at a different pace, had there been a revolutionary party to intervene.

THE OTHER arm of the state's repressive power, the police, were as deeply disaffected as the army.

The government had not treated its servants well. Pay was poor, hours long, and the militaristic police hierarchy highly oppressive. Any faintest sign of disaffection was stamped on by dismissal or transfer to another station. Influenced by the big labour unrest of 1910-14 and the leap in trade union membership, the police too formed their own union in October 1913. The National Union of Police and Prison Officers (NUPPO) was initially centred mainly in London.

The Commissioner of the Metropolitan Police, Sir Edward Henry, immediately made it clear that any officer joining the union was liable for dismissal and the union would not be recognised.[1] This was extended in 1916 to cover any policeman even attending union meetings.[2]

The union consequently led a clandestine life, causing some amusing incidents. When the military police raided one police union meeting in February 1917, the look-out on the door gave warning as they clattered up the stairs, and the door was held shut while the married men escaped out of the window and down the fire escape. The names of forty policemen were taken, of whom fourteen were dismissed the force and the rest heavily fined.

1918 saw a growing number of strikes — London bus conductresses, Lancashire millworkers, Welsh railwaymen and Yorkshire miners being examples — all of which resulted in improvements for the workers. NUPPO was drawn into this rising wave of industrial struggle and established firm links with the London Trades Council, on which six of its men served.[3] When Police Constable Tommy Thiel was dismissed on 25 August 1918 for organising the union in the provinces, the NUPPO executive drew up an ultimatum demanding better pay, the reinstatement of Thiel, and recognition of the union. It also suspended a 'no strike' clause of its constitution, and called a strike for midnight on 29 August.

In April 1917 the union had had only 47 paid-up members in the Metropolitan and City forces. The chairman, James Marston, was confident, however, that between four and five thousand would answer the call to strike. In the event, ten to twelve thousand of the Met's 19,000-strong force came out.[4] The city centre was solid, the outlying districts were patchy. Even Special Branch men were affected. At Scotland Yard 25 sergeants and 16 constables stopped work. Thousands of new members joined the union.[5] The London Trades Council agreed to support the police union by every means within its power.

The method of getting the 100 per cent turn-out in the inner areas also looks amusing today. Flying mass pickets, sometimes over 600-strong, went to all stations. They searched them inside and out to see there were no men on duty, broke up parades if they were taking place, and manhandled resisters. At one station a constable insisted on reporting for duty. 'Within seconds his helmet was torn off and, his arms firmly held, he was dragged off with the crowd . . .'[6]

A vast, triumphant demonstration was held at Tower Hill.

What could Lloyd George do? — 'The war probably going on for another year; industrial unrest throughout the country; police in the capital city in a state of mutiny and in virtual control of Whitehall; the only soldiers available young recruits, many of them known to be sympathetic to the police claims.[7]

He sent the president of NUPPO, the union he had spurned and refused to consult, to find the union chairman with a request to meet him at Downing Street next day.

No sooner had the meeting at Downing Street started on 31 August when a message came informing the prime minister that the soldiers outside, brought in to replace the striking police guards, were fraternising with the masses of police strikers outside and openly saying they would refuse to obey any order to clear them from the streets or break the strike.

Lloyd George had little option but to capitulate. He raised higher the already increased Home Office pay offer, introduced a widows' pension, reinstated Thiel and all the others — a score or so — dismissed for union activity. The dejected Sir Edward Henry moaned: 'They actually got more than they asked for.'[8] Years later Lloyd George said: 'This country was nearer to Bolshevism that day than at any time since.'[9]

The police returned to duty 44 hours after the start of the strike with a famous victory under their belt.

But Lloyd George the wily Welshman was not to be out-smarted. He defused the situation sufficiently to gain time to put the knife into the heart of the police demand — recognition of the union. At the meeting on 31 August he made a cryptic remark: 'The government cannot recognise a union for the police *in wartime*.' This disoriented the union, for they believed that the union would be recognised after the war.

After the strike Lloyd George jettisoned the inadequate Commissioner of the Metropolitan Police and brought in Nevil Macready, a whizzkid of Tonypandy notoriety. During the 1910 miners' strike at Tonypandy in South Wales, he had become well-known for having deployed small numbers of troops to clear the side streets by prodding the strikers with their bayonets — where it made it hard for them to sit down afterwards.[10]

The union now grew by leaps and bounds, reaching 55,000 in June 1919. It won further concessions against autocratic authority, got into line with other unions in seeking the eight-hour day, and affiliated to the TUC. It also held big demonstrations — up to 9,000-strong — in the Albert Hall, Trafalgar Square and Hyde Park.

Unable to stamp out the union immediately, Macready intro-duced on 12 September 1918 what he was to build up as the alternative to the union, namely the Police Representative Boards.

Key to its constitution was that it was 'to be entirely unassociated with any outside body' — meaning the TUC or any other Labour organisations, in other words it should not become an independent union.

NUPPO accepted this as the war was still on, but it expected to replace the Boards afterwards. Then to Macready's dismay it proceeded systematically to take over the Boards. The union's widely-read **Police and Prison Officers' Magazine**, which was published from 19 December 1918 to 20 November 1919, stated categorically: '. . . the Representative Board must, of necessity, be leading Union members, so the name "Representative Board" is merely camouflage for "The National Union of Police and Prison Officers".'[11]

Union members entirely succeeded at the elections in the Metropolitan area on 5 October 1918, forcing Macready to rethink. For the next elections in March 1919 he arranged that the three ranks of constables, sergeants and inspectors should be separated, each electing their own Board. He also made careful preparations for future police strikes, paying particular attention to the most important police stations, arranging for small squads of military to move speedily to support blacklegs, and for army despatch riders in case telephone lines were cut.[12]

On the secondary issues of pay and conditions he followed his master, Lloyd George, and conceded improvements. Lloyd George himself dangled a carrot in the form of the Desborough Committee, one of his many Committees of Inquiry or Commissions of 1919, which kept the talking going till the steam ran out. This committee was to play an important part in holding off the second police strike and eventually enervating it through big concessions. He cleverly included two leading trade unionists in it, James Sexton and James O'Grady, both Labour MPs.

The union threw out Macready's scheme for three separate Boards and boycotted the elections in March, succeeding in almost preventing voting for the constables' board, but being less successful with the higher ranks.

By the end of March Lloyd George's tactics on the industrial front had succeeded, and the strike pressure from the miners and other key sectors of industry had receded for the time being. The government could therfore go in for the kill on the police, whose loyal services they were still to need.

On 30 May Macready issued Orders, previously used against the Glasgow tramwaymen during the Forty Hours Strike in January and February, which included a draconian threat of dismissal *and* total loss of pension to anyone who went on strike, even if under intimidation.[13] After one of the union's divisional secretaries caved in to this threat and gave up the union, its executive decided to act quickly before demoralisation should set in. At the beginning of June it organised a strike ballot over the demand for union recognition and the reinstatement of a sacked member. This resulted in a massive vote of 48,863 for and 4,324 against a strike.[14]

The government reacted by speeding up the Desborough Committee. Its concessions on pay and conditions, together with Macready's threat, rapidly dissipated the strike support. The union meanwhile, becoming despondent about support for a strike within the police, assiduously sought support from the industrial trade unions. Marston, the president, and Hayes, the secretary, tirelessly travelled up and down the country. They got support — in words — and Hayes wrote thanking the miners, railwaymen, transport workers, dockers, steel and iron workers, boot and shoe operatives, cotton operatives, building trades, engineers, general workers, government employees, etc., etc.

But the miners, railwaymen and transport workers had failed to strike on their own behalf. Would they do so for the police? Hot air was the order of the day in those summer months after the retreat of the miners; there was plenty of talk of direct action in the big unions — and no action.

Lloyd George, who knew how to be generous when the pressures on him were dangerously strong, had no need for that now. He wanted to kill the union once and for all and cease to worry about police loyalty. He finally provoked the strike by snubbing a police deputation.[15] Marston later told the TUC: 'The government forced the issue at their own time, and the police themselves had not the slightest discretion in the matter. They were obliged to fight at this time, or else never fight at all.'[16]

The strike took place on 31 July and dragged on for about a week. Only 1,081 came out in London, 1,600 in Liverpool and 112 in Birmingham.[17] Many NUPPO executive members failed to strike. Out of all the promises of help from other trade unions, only the Nine Elms Branch of the National Union of Railwaymen, 750-strong, came out in sympathy, and Jimmy Thomas, general secretary of the NUR, soon pushed them back. The successful tactics of the previous year — bursting into stations to flush men out — failed; Macready had organised resistance.

London stayed calm. But Liverpool, where half the men were out, experienced the worst rioting ever seen, for three days and nights. A battleship and two destroyers were sent to the Mersey, and the army brought in to restore order.

All the strikers were dismissed and never reinstated, despite Labour Party Conference and TUC resolutions, and three Labour governments, two under Ramsay Macdonald, who, with Arthur Henderson, had pledged recognition to the union, and one under Attlee, who had after the strike campaigned hard for reinstatement. When Labour came to power, they forgot their pledges. They needed a loyal police force, just like any other capitalist government. Marston joined the Communist Party; Hayes became a Labour MP.

The government learnt the danger of undervaluing its servants, and ever after made sure they had good pay and conditions. That much the union achieved for the police. Contrariwise, in doing so, it ensured that from then on the police force would be the state's wholly loyal bully boys.

But since then we have not yet had a repetition of the semi-revolutionary conditions of 1919 to destabilise the forces of the state.

THE FORTY HOURS STRIKE

THE KEY to the semi-revolutionary nature of the situation in 1919 was the activity of the working class at the point of production. The strike wave rose unremittingly towards the end of the war and after it. Strikes inspired more strikes in a ceaseless tide of militancy and solidarity.

What made the situation pregnant with revolutionary potential were the threats of the big battalions of the working class: the engineers on the Clyde, talking of calling a general strike, and, at the very heart of the economy, the million-strong army of the miners, backed by the Triple Alliance, whose other members were the railway and transport unions, all of whom were at the time clamouring for a resolution to their separate claims. If they all came out, as they threatened to do, the government could not have weathered the storm, as it would not have found enough reliable troops and police to suppress by violence a national upsurge of such dimensions.

However, coordinated strike action on such a big scale does not arise spontaneously. Working-class unity has to be fought and campaigned for by a party of organised revolutionary socialists. And there *were* active revolutionaries in Britain at this time.

On Clydeside and in Sheffield members of the Socialist Labour Party such as Arthur MacManus and J T Murphy had led major wartime strikes of engineers. John Maclean had won an international reputation for his revolutionary opposition to the war. In mining the South Wales Unofficial Reform Committee had a powerful base of support, while Maclean had some influence in the

Lanarkshire coalfield. Even on the railways, not noted for a history of militancy, an extensive network of unofficial 'Vigilance Committees' subjected the union officials to intense rank-and-file pressure.

Alas, these revolutionary currents were no more unified in organisation or action than the class as a whole. Politics, like nature, abhors a vacuum. And in the cirumstances of 1919 the only centralised force in the labour movement was the trade union officials. Though tiny in number they became the most influential factor in the crisis.

The potential for united class action existed in such bodies as the Triple Alliance, but since no one challenged the officials for its leadership, the Alliance became a means of holding the most powerful section of the organised working class back from the action towards which they were straining. As 1919 unfolded, the lack of an organised revolutionary alternative was to cripple the struggle for socialism at every turn. But at the start of the year the situation was still highly upredictable. The historian Allen Hutt comments: 'at such a time of extreme social tension the first volley fired would have sounded the death knell of the regime even more surely than the volleys of Bloody Sunday in Petersburg introduced Russia's 1905 upheaval.'[1]

The Cabinet's daily meetings dealt with not much else than the strike situation and the spectre of 'Bolshevism'. For instance, the Cabinet meeting on Friday 31 January dealt with the strikes in Belfast and Glasgow, the demands (and threats) of coalminers, the 'Railway Situation', where the men were 'in some measure out of hand, and although they had been instructed by their leaders to observe . . . the agreement, it could not be guaranteed that they would do so,' and the coming tube strike.[2]

The next Cabinet meeting, on Monday 3 February, dealt with seven items. Six were about different strikes, and to add to fears of the spreading of the huge Glasgow strike for the 40-hour week came gloomy 'indications that the miners and railwaymen generally might strike in the course of the week.'[3] The secretary of state for Scotland declared that 'it was more clear than ever that it was a misnomer to call the situation in Glasgow a strike — it was a Bolshevist rising.' The President of the Board of Trade concluded that 'it was important that the Glasgow trouble should subside before entering upon a new conflict with labour.' Sir Eric Geddes, minister of reconstruction and later to earn a reputation as a 'troubleshooter', put on a show of bravado: 'It was suggested that a big general strike was probably coming sooner or later, and if and when it came the strike would be on the ground chosen by the government.'[4]

How much worse could things get if even 'The King is in a funk about the labour situation and is talking about the . . . danger of a revolution', as Bonar Law said to Lloyd George.[5]

The target of all the demands was the government. Even though mines, railways, docks, munitions works, and so on were privately owned, the government had taken over control for the duration of the war and was thus, as Austin Chamberlain remarked, the 'ultimate arbiter in labour disputes'.[6] It thus had a total picture of the situation and its guardianship of capitalist class interests was carried out in a highly centralised manner.

A centralised leadership of the working class, symmetrical to that of the ruling class and therefore able to challenge it, did not exist. The workers entered the arena through their trade unions. But trade unions are by definition sectional, being the organisations of circumstantially different groups of workers, each pursuing its own claims in its own time according to its own traditions and without reference to others. So while the unions unite workers, they also separate them from one another. Being defensive organisations of the working class within the capitalist system, they cannot lead the working class to socialism. The smashing of the state and introduction of workers' control needs the guidance of a party which acts inside the trade unions to push them along a revolutionary road as far as they are capable of going, and at the same time surmounts their sectionalism in a united, self-conscious bid for political power.

The advantage in the class struggle in early 1919 lay with the workers. Nevertheless at the end of three months of the greatest working-class ferment, the government still emerged the victor. We shall sketch the course of the Glasgow strike, the Forty Hours Strike, as it was called, and the coal and railway negotiations, to see how the governent rode the storm of these three mighty and crucial working-class battles.

The Forty Hours Strike was the highest point of a class struggle in which Glasgow had been in the vanguard during the war. Engineering was the major industry on the Clyde, employing a quarter of a million, one third of all its workers.[7] During the Labour Unrest before the war engineering workers had fought big battles against their employers. The unions had become strongly entrenched, quadrupling in membership between 1910 and 1920,[8] with four of every five workers in unions, mainly in the Amalgamated Society of Engineers (ASE). These battles were led by a committee of delegates from the participating factories. A strong tradition of militant rank-and-file leadership was thus forged which enjoyed the confidence of the workforce.

The war widened the cleavage between the official and rank-and-file leaderships within the unions. The officials became completely absorbed into the chauvinist tide in support of the war: they agreed to the Munitions Act of 1915, under which they readily signed away for the duration of the war normal trade union practices and the right to strike (the exception was the miners' union). The militant shop stewards, on the other hand, were not so ready to knuckle under.

The agreements made by the union officials allowed the 'dilution' of labour. This meant that work which had previously been classified as skilled could now be given to unskilled workers. For the government and employers to get the maximum benefit from this, the old craft method of one man seeing a job through from beginning to end was broken down into separate tasks, each of which was — in management's eyes — more suitable for an unskilled worker. This brought a 'conveyor belt' type of division of labour, radically socialising the production process.

The contradiction within the workings of the capitalist system, which was producing 'competitive anarchy' abroad in the trenches and socialised production at home,[9] was not lost on the leading shop stewards with their radical socialist traditions, and strengthened their revolutionary Marxist views. Reformism, expressed basically as the conscious separation of politics and economics, thus had a weaker impact in Scotland than in England. The militants could see the connection between the political sphere, the war, and the economic, the changes in the factories. The revolutionary left therefore, though small, was able to have a stronger impact.

This was important in the development on the Clyde of the significant anti-war movement and the big strike movement (unofficial of course) from 1915 onwards. There was action over both economic issues, for example the 'twopence strike' of 1915, and political issues, such as the strike against the Munitions Act later the same year. Out of this movement was born the Clyde Workers' Committee (CWC).

The Clyde Workers' Committee was made up of shop stewards from the striking factories, all of whom were socialists.[10] Between 250 and 300 shop stewards, representing tens of thousands of workers, met each week for a little over a year, and led whatever strikes took place in the engineering industry.

With the abrupt end of the war on 11 November 1918, brought about by a workers' revolution in Germany — a revolution applauded at a demonstration of 30,000 Clydesiders[11] — the hunger for munitions ceased and the engineers were faced with the problems both of unemployment (up to 11 per cent in February 1919)[12] and the absorption of demobilised workers. The CWC, which had ceased to exist from 1916, revived. As a solution to the two problems it proposed a radical reduction in working hours — the average was then 54 hours a week. The CWC emulated the miners in calling for a 30-hour week: 'Six hours per day, five days per week, £1 per day minimum . . . Working-class solidarity means you stand where the miners stand.'[13]

On 5 January the CWC set up a 'Ways and Means Committee' of eight to bring all the shop stewards in the area together with a mandate from their respective workshops in the hope of taking united action over the issue of working hours.

But while there was a move throughout the working class for shorter hours, the figure to be attached varied section by section, union by union and even among sections of the same union. Thus in early January the arguments over the figure divided the movement roughly as follows:

For 47 hours: the ASE Executive, which claimed confirmation by a ballot with a 2:1 majority.

For 44 hours: Belfast had a general strike for this demand simultaneously with Glasgow.

For 40 hours (at least): the Glasgow district committee of the ASE and the local membership of the skilled engineering unions; also the Scottish Labour Party, ILP and Scottish TUC. A major factor in pushing for the 40-hour week was Emmanuel Shinwell, the president and major force of the Glasgow Trades Council.

For 30 hours: the CWC's Ways and Means Committee.

The workshop union branch votes divided as follows: for 30 hours, 104; for 40 hours, 83; for 47 hours, 13; neutral, 1.

From early January the different bodies wrestled to take the initiative from one another on the hours issue.[14] The arguments over the demand continued through meeting after meeting, and would have continued right up to 25 January, two days before the strike, when the Scottish TUC's normal timetable would have enabled it to make a decision, had not Shinwell forestalled this at a conference called by the CWC on 18 January, by carrying a proposal for a joint committee representing all the interests, official and unofficial.[15] On this he managed to get through, by a vote of 27 to 18, agreement on a strike for a 40-hour week.[16]

Shinwell chaired the joint committee, and Willie Gallacher was elected strike organiser. The committee consisted of the Ways and Means Committee of the CWC, the Parliamentary Committee of the Scottish TUC, the Glasgow Trades Council, the district committees of the Ship and Allied Trades and other individual unions, including the district committee of the ASE.

The mixture of unofficial and official bodies differentiated the Forty Hours Strike from the previous wartime strikes on the

34

Clyde. Those had been completely unofficial and led by the engineering shop stewards of the CWC. The dimensions of this strike were larger — the concept was that of a general strike embracing workers well beyond the engineers — and the CWC felt this required the leadership of other trade union bodies, whose rank-and-file organisation was not so well-developed as the engineers'. The powerful unofficial organisation of the engineers was therefore not in full control of the strike. The extension of leadership brought only a limited extension of the strike to other workers, and failed to bring out the unskilled workers, while the official trade union bodies hindered the committed, energetic prosecution of the strike.

The date fixed for the strike was 27 January. As this approached, enthusiasm among some of the official bodies waned rather than waxed. In fact, the only reason they stayed on the committee was in order not to lose control over their members. The Parliamentary Committee had initially been dragged onto the committee through its desire to prevent a 30-hour strike. Now it 'considered the action of calling a General Strike on Monday 27th January hasty and unwise.'[17] Only the casting vote of its chairman (who happened also to be secretary of the Glasgow Trades Council) kept the Parliamentary Committee's delegate on the committee and the Parliamentary Committee in support.[18] The ASE district committee was embarrassed by going against its union executive, but its greater worry about leaving its members under the control of others triumphed.[19] It was this desperate anxiety not to lose control which finally brought agreement on the forty hours and kept the joint committee together.

This sectionalism in the original formulation of the demand was compounded by the sectionalism in carrying it out, with groups of workers who had originally supported the call falling out either before or soon after the strike began. The joint committee proved unable to spread the strike much beyond that group of workers which had carried out the big wartime strikes — the engineers — even though the demand was a general one for all workers. It was the engineers who suffered most from unemployment, and they with whom friction accumulated over the working of the 47-hour week which had been introduced in engineering and shipbuilding on 1 January. The joint committee even failed to notify the National Committee of Shop Stewards of its plans or seek its support, sending delegates to other towns for this purpose only after the strike's fifth day, Bloody Friday, 31 January.[20]

The strike Manifesto named the unions of the dock labourers, horse and motormen, railwaymen, municipal employees, building trades and electricians as being involved,[21] but the dockers withdrew to negotiate separately for a 44-hour week, the horse and motormen succumbed to a separate offer of a reduction in their working week of 14½ hours,[22] the municipal employees never struck at all, partly through the traditional rivalry between unskilled workers and the skilled engineers,[23] but mostly no doubt because the government threatened the tramway workers with dismissal and loss of pension rights if they did.

Only the electricians eventually supported the strike wholeheartedly.[24] They threatened to strike in London too on 6 February. The leaders of the National Union of Scottish Mineworkers declared that they 'entirely dissociated themselves from the present erratic strike movement,'[25] and were hard at it trying to get striking Fife miners back to work. But the Lanarkshire miners came out in solidarity after 1,500 rank-and-file miners occupied the offices of their executive, forcing it to toe the line.[26] Yet the strenuous efforts of the miners' executive succeeded in the end, and nearly all the miners were back at work after the first week of the fortnight's strike.[27]

Another factor preventing the strike from achieving its full potential was the pressure to keep politics out of it. The Manifesto drawn up by Shinwell said: 'This movement . . . is not revolutionary in character, nor is it inspired by the legitimate demand for more leisure. It is attributable solely and entirely to the fear of possible unemployment in the near future and the desire of the workers generally to make room for demobilised servicemen.'[28]

At the mass meeting on the first day of the strike the joint committee issued strict instructions that no speaker be allowed the use of the platform unless he was a striker; 'the object of such instructions being to keep the political element entirely outside,' observes D S Morton, one of the joint committee's secretaries.[29] Gallacher, in his book **Revolt on the Clyde**, written in 1936, reflects on the strike leaders' deficiencies: '. . . for those of us who were leading the strike, we were strike leaders, nothing more; we had forgotten we were revolutionary leaders of the working class . . . We were carrying on a strike when we ought to have been making a revolution.'[30]

Yet despite all this — 'the condition of our leadership, no plan, no unity of purpose, watching one another and waiting for and wondering what was going to happen'[31] — the response of the workers was magnificent. 40,000 came out on 27 January, and the strike spread daily, reaching up to 100,000. Belfast had come out a couple of days earlier, on 25 January, in a general, unofficial strike for the 44-hour week, even more widespread than Glasgow, with gas, electricity and tramway workers joining in, cutting off all lighting, much heat and power, and bringing the industrial life of the city to a standstill.[32] A telegram from Belfast to the Cabinet stated: 'The workmen have formed a "Soviet" Committee, and this Committee had received 47 applications from small traders for permission to use light.'[33] The two towns were in daily communication, giving heart to each other.[34] Belfast also went back later than Glasgow, on 19 January. The strike also spread to 14,000 workers in Edinburgh. A daily Strike Bulletin was produced, and sold 20,000 copies a day.

The strike was conducted with enormous energy. The workers were involved in mass meetings every day. From the second day mass pickets five to ten thousand-strong marched from factory to factory. They lined up outside working enterprises leaving a narrow channel through which the workers had individually to run the gauntlet.[35] Strikers' wives were closely involved in picketing besides other activities, and 'we have had as many as five thousand females forming one of our massed pickets,' says Morton.[36] By the third day, Wednesday 29 January, all factories were closed.[37]

A massive picket attempted to get the power stations closed. The private ones did close, and one of the two Corporation stations, but Pinkston, supplying power to the trams, did not. Instead the men were given board and lodging in the station by the employers, and a company of troops by the authorities as protection.

On Wednesday 29th a deputation went to the Lord Provost of Glasgow to ask him to seek government intervention, and a mass meeting was called to hear the result on Friday 31st. The government, strongly protesting that it was not intervening, weighed up the situation in Cabinet, and decided to use maximum force, for reasons we shall analyse later.

The massive demonstration of 35,000 in George Square on 31 January was brutally attacked by the police. Kirkwood, a strike leader, was batoned unconscious, and Gallacher wounded. That night six tanks and 100 motor lorries were sent north to Glasgow and occupied the city, reinforcing a massive deployment of young raw army recruits from England and Scotland (outside Glasgow). Soldiers at the local barracks at Maryhill were kept strictly indoors and inactive, and the strikers, as Gallacher later regrets, failed to approach and fraternise with them and seek their assistance.[38] Morton says the soldiers had no idea of their purpose or destination and some were amazed when informed by the pickets that they were in Glasgow.

On Saturday 1 February Glasgow was an armed camp, occupied by troops with bayonets, machine guns, tanks and aeroplanes. Gallacher, Kirkwood, Shinwell and others were arrested and sentenced three months later, Shinwell to five months in jail, Gallacher to three months, with Kirkwood acquitted.

Despite attempts by the National Committee of Shop Stewards later in the day to spread the strike, the national union officials succeeded in preventing this. In fact the ASE, after consultation with the government, suspended its Glasgow and Belfast district committees on 6 February. The strike was ended six days later.

The strike succeeded in speeding up the reduction of hours worked, and contributed to preserving and improving wage levels. The government had extricated itself from this first big battle on the industrial front by using force as a supplement to the control of the workers by the trade union bureaucracy.

4

THE GOVERNMENT'S panic measures in Glasgow had their root in fears from another quarter — a national strike by the million miners, agitation for which came to a head in the first two months of the year. Behind the miners loomed the spectre of the Triple Alliance, an alliance formed during the war between miners, railwaymen and transport workers, each partner of which, while acting independently, had a moral obligation to back the other two in a dispute. Its potential power was enormous, and the danger of a conflagration imminent, as all three had wage claims in at the same time in January and February.

Coal mining was another key industry on which the war industry had depended, and the miners, like the engineers, had taken advantage of their pivotal position to advance their claims by a high level of industrial militancy. As early in the war as July 1915, 200,000 South Wales miners struck.[1] In May 1918, 50,000 miners struck, in August 60,000.[2]

The dawn of 1919 saw a continuing struggle. In the week ending 14 January 1919 there were 18 new miners' strikes,[3] the next week 20 new ones.[4] The week afterwards saw the settlement of many large strikes: of 150,000 Yorkshire miners who had been out for 13 days,[5] of 50,000 Nottinghamshire and Derbyshire miners, of 12,000 in Fifeshire, several thousand in West Lothian. And these were mostly unofficial. 'The strikes,' remarks the Ministry of Labour, 'have not usually been undertaken with the sanction of the trade unions.'[6]

The miners won consistently. With the government's bottomless appetite for coal to keep industry going during the war, and the critically low coal stocks in the immediate aftermath — a boom period for a couple of years — the miners constituted a militant, self-confident, formidable power to be reckoned with.

Their demands were presented to the government on a number of occasions, the '9th January, 12th January and 15th January,' a Miners' Executive member who was also an MP complained irritably, and were 'talked about as long ago as August and September 1918.'[7] A Special Conference of the Miners' Federation of Great Britain (MFGB), held at Southport on 14 January, packaged the demands, whose three main elements were: a 30 per cent wage increase, a reduction of working hours from eight to six per day, and nationalisation of the industry with joint control by owners and miners.[8] This last demand was an age-old dream passed in principle at Trade Union Congresses 42 times since 1882, and, specifically relating to mining, for 20 years.[9] Now, for the first time, with the ferment in the working class and the miners consistently triumphant, it was actually capable of being realised.

The miners' claim was an explosive mixture of economic and political demands. During those early months of 1919 in Britain, as in Russia, Germany, Hungary and so many other countries, the revolutionary urge to smash capitalism overrode and drew in its wake the myriad economic demands of the workers. So the dream of ending coal capitalism, now really within the grasp of the miners, inspired their insistence on fighting for a better life all round.

The miners' demands were discussed with the government on Friday 31 January,[10] with the threat that unless a reply was received by the following Monday, 3 February, 'trouble would ensue . . .'[11]

The government had its back to the wall. Besides the army and police unrest and the near-general strikes in Glasgow and Belfast, there was an alarming escalation of other strikes, threats of strikes and fears of solidarity strikes. At a Cabinet meeting on 6 February, which discussed the London tube and Southern Railway strike of 8,000 men[12] that had started three days earlier, the

40

Postmaster General was for being tough, and said: 'If any concessions were made now, it would only be the prelude to further lightning strikes, more especially in the postal services,' and he was 'in favour of fighting the battle right through.'[13] On the other hand, Sir Herbert Walker, chairman of the Railway Executive, called for concessions: 'Unless this [demand] was accepted the strike would certainly extend over the Firemen's Union, and possibly over the National Union of Railwaymen,' he said, and 'admitted that they were skating on thin ice.'[14]

In preparation for the threatened electrical strike on 6 February, the Cabinet decided to arrest three or four of its leaders. This horrified the secretary of state for Home Affairs: 'If the busmen heard that leaders of the electric strike had been arrested this might cause the busmen to come out.'[15]

The revolutionary potential of these strikes was apparent to the government. Churchill three months later recalls this period in order to justify the 'Circular to Commanders' which was issued at this time:

> Let us look back upon the circumstances in which this document was drafted. It was at the end of January last, if I rightly recollect. The situation then was extraordinarily difficult. We had a considerable number of mutinies in the Army . . . We had a number of strikes and a great many threats of strikes. There was a threatened railway strike, and the actual strike which took place all over the tube railways in London. There was a threatened strike of the electricians, which was averted only at the last moment. There were serious riots in Glasgow, which required the presence of a large number of troops. There was the threatened strike of the Triple Alliance . . .[16]

The First Lord of the Admiralty expressed his panic more starkly. On 5 February he said:

> . . . unless we acted soon, the situation would become worse and worse each day. There was no doubt that we were up against a Bolshevist movment in London, Glasgow and elsewhere. He had just returned from one of the naval ports where

there had been a little trouble, which was purely of a Bolshevist nature.[17]

Basil Home Thomson, soon to be Director of Intelligence at the Home Office, said:

During the first three months of 1919 unrest touched its high-water mark. I do not think that at any time in history since the Bristol Riots we have been so near revolution . . . On the 27th of January there were extensive strikes on the Clyde of a revolutionary rather than an economic character.[18]

A Labour MP feelingly summed up the situation, referring

to the industrial unrest and social discontent that is seething like a mad whirlpool around us . . . When you come to consider the world-wide upheaval and unrest expressing itself in the fullest terms in revolutonary action in all parts of the world any sane man, bending his mind to the thought of the present, must realise that action, commenced in quite an innocent way, may be like a match applied to a powder magazine.[19]

The Cabinet had to decide how to avoid catastrophe. First, it carefully analysed the miners' crucial strengths in any confrontation. In a Memorandum to the Cabinet the minister of labour, Sir Robert Horne, dealt with the development of national as opposed to local negotiations, the congruence of pit, lodge and community, the miners' past industrial successes, and the centrality of coal to the economy — a combination of which the government had good cause to be afraid.

The Miners' Federation has for a considerable time been consolidating its position . . . and now is very strong, apart even from the unique position afforded by the pivotal character of the industry. Thus, during the war membership has been increased, and, more important than this, organisation has been tightened with a view to national as opposed to local negotiations with employers . . . during the war this principle was conceded by the Coal Controller, and the Federation has now decided to allow no local wage settlements without its consent.

42

Other circumstances also place the miners in a peculiarly strong position, even among the great pivotal industries. Thus, the nature of the work performed tends to separate them from other workers and to throw them very much together themselves. The results of this have been seen on occasion in their comparatively small susceptibility to public opinion. Again, it is a fact that at the present time they can look back on a practically unbroken series of successes won during the war over employers and the Government by strikes or threat of strikes . . .

But, of course, the main strength of the position of the miners lies in the almost unique importance of the industry. In other industries, when the resources of conciliation have been exhausted, it may be possible for the Government to face a strike. In the great pivotal industries, and especially in the coalmining industry in circumstances such as the present, this is extremely difficult . . . There is, then, every reason to suppose that the miners mean to make the most of the situation which presents itself at the moment, and such a determination undoubtedly presents an extremely difficult problem for the Government to deal with.[20]

He thought the present claims 'might only be regarded as an "affair of outposts"; the big battle would be joined later . . . The moral he would draw was that the Government must take immediate steps to develop their plans in order to meet a much more serious situation later.'

Sir Adrian Nimmo, adviser to the Coal Controller, was too alarmed to wait for 'later'; '. . . the minister of labour might be correct in stating that the big battle was to come later, but his own information was to the effect that the miners in South Wales, at any rate, were out for a fight now.'[21]

The arguments in the Cabinet, and their outcome, veered as usual between carrot and stick. On 4 February 1919 the Cabinet appointed an Industrial Unrest Committee 'to make the necessary arrangements for dealing with any situation that might arise from industrial unrest both at the present moment and in the future.'[22]

On 6 February it decided the Ministry of Labour could spend what it required for propaganda purposes 'during the present industrial unrest.'[23]

On 7 February the Cabinet reconstituted the wartime network of government spies in all areas of the country to inform on militants and socialists, with the particular brief to examine and report on 'why there was so much revolt against the authority of the trade unions' — meaning the trade union leaders.[24] The spying was done on a grand scale, intelligence officers all over the country submitting reports *twice daily* which resulted in first-hand early information being obtained from sources other than those at the disposal of government offices concerned.[25] The **Daily Herald** of 17 May wrote of a vast system of espionage in the ranks of labour.[26] The information was collated by Basil Home Thomson, head of the Special Branch, in a Memorandum to the Cabinet called 'Fortnightly Report on Revolutionary Organisations in the United Kingdom and Morale Abroad'. In April 1919, the Home Office established a Directorate of Intelligence which published weekly summaries under the title 'Report on Revolutionary Organisations in the United Kingdom'.[27] Thomson became its director. This was in addition to a weekly Ministry of Labour Memorandum which also informed on the industrial scene and the left press.

On 11 February, on the eve of a Special MFGB Conference, the prime minister bluffed and blustered in a threatening speech in the House of Commons; intent upon fighting

> . . . any demand which is pressed forward with a view not to obtaining fair conditions, but with ulterior motives — to hold up and to overthrow the existing order and to destroy Government, relying not upon the justice of the claim, but the brute force which is behind it . . . we are determined to fight Prussianism in the industrial world . . . with the whole might of the nation.[28]

Undeterred, the Miners' Special Conference decided to ballot its members. The prime minister feared the worst — quite correctly, as the ballot result, announced on 25 February, was 615,164 to 105,082 for a strike. There were pleas from some of his Cabinet to be 'as generous as possible . . . it was worthwhile paying something to avoid the threatening catastrophe'[29] for, according to the minister of labour, 'if the coal miners would not strike the railwaymen would continue their negotiations. But if the coal miners struck the railwaymen would strike also.'[30]

A strike of the Triple Alliance was the greatest threat of all. Jimmy Thomas, leader of the NUR and so also one of the Triple Alliance leaders, rattled his sabre menacingly in the House of Commons after he knew the miners' ballot result:

> The position of the miners, railwaymen, and transport workers' executives this afternoon . . . was given unanimously that no one section was to settle this question without consultation and agreement with the others. That decision means that the miners will conduct their negotiations . . . the railwaymen will reopen their negotiations tomorrow, and then the transport workers will resume theirs. But no one of these three bodies will be in a position to make a separate agreeement without a further conference of the whole three, and that conference is fixed to be held before the 1st March.

And if that weren't enough:

> . . . however difficult an official strike may be, a non-official strike will be worse, because there is always the grave danger in unofficial strikes of no one being able to control them . . .
> There are people . . . who know perfectly well that the conflict if it comes will be the most terrible that we can contemplate, and the responsibility on any man is terrible.

So, Lloyd George, you had better preserve our credibility and deliver concessions — Thomas was saying — so that we can hold our members back from striking!

> Now it is for the Government to strengthen the hands of those who desire peace and who are striving for peace . . . no Labour leader with any sense of responsibility would face the consequences of such a struggle as this with other than a very heavy heart.[31]

There was no way the government could storm in on this situation as it had in Glasgow. It may threaten, but it had to appear to be delivering something. The carrot it offered the miners was a Royal Commission under Mr Justice Sankey to inquire into wages, hours and conditions in the pits and 'any scheme . . . for the future organisation of the coal industry, whether on the present basis, or on the basis of joint control, nationalisation, or any other basis.' The miners were given the unprecedented inducement of nominating or approving half the members of the Commission, excluding the chairman. The prime minister had already managed to delay considering the miners' claims for nearly two months; if the Commission were accepted the talk could go on and on, while the revolutionary steam would hopefully be blown off.

In an attempt to make assurance double sure, Lloyd George adopted a second stratagem to gain time. Amid great publicity he set up a National Industrial Conference of employers and workers which met at the Central Hall, Westminster, on 27 February to consider the causes of industrial unrest and what remedies could be proposed. The government made an impressive show at the highest level, putting the minister of labour, Robert Horne, in the chair, and the prime minister himself addressing the conference. A number of unions accepted the invitation to participate, although the Triple Alliance and the engineers refused. On 4 April its report was published. It recommended a maximum 48-hour week, the establishment of a minimum wage, and the setting up of a Council and Standing Committee to advise the government.

The government's cynical bluff regarding its brainchild was clearly exposed at the Cabinet meeting of 3 April, 24 hours before the report became public:

> The Minister of Labour said that on the previous day he had seen a leading employer, who had arrived at the conclusion that the country had been so near the precipice within the last few weeks that the only way to convince Labour that the Government was sympathetic was to accept the Report and introduce the necessary legislation as soon as possible.

As against this,

> The Chancellor of the Exchequer said that, supposing it was right to accept the Report, to do so at 24 hours' notice would

have a very damaging effect, and when the necessary legislation was being introduced, the fact that the Government had accepted the Report at such short notice, and without careful digestion, would tell against them in the House of Commons.[32]

Lloyd George sided with the Minister of Labour, sensing the importance of continuing the bluff; and he called the two resulting Bills presented to parliament on maximum hours and minimum wages in August 1919 'the most important measures dealing with Labour problems which have ever been submitted to the judgment of this House.'[33] After this trumpeting, the Bills were quietly buried, as was the National Industrial Conference Committee itself two years later — 'unwept, unhonoured, and unsung'.

The Labour Party set great store by the National Industrial Conference. Its Executive Report to the Labour Party Conference spoke in favour of Sankey and the National Industrial Conference: '. . . both these inquiries have exerted a considerable influence in allaying, at any rate temporarily, the widespread feeling of industrial discontent which was so serious and threatening a factor in our national life in recent months.'[34] That, indeed, was precisely the tactic of the government: to pass the point of greatest danger in safety.

The offer of the Sankey Commission was seen by masses of miners, with their hardened realism, for the deception it was. A Labour MP spoke of 'the suggestion . . . which is being assiduously circulated in the mining districts that the Government propose this Committee for the purpose of indefinitely delaying a settlement.'[35] Sylvia Pankhurst's paper, **Workers' Dreadnought**, asked: 'Has not a Government inquiry become the classical method of leaving things the way they are?'[36] Writing of the feeling in South Wales, miners' MP Ness Edwards recalled 'that it was generally felt by the active rank and file elements that this Sankey Commission was merely a tactic of the Government to put off the evil day of the trial of strength between demands for workers' control and the retention of private enterprise.'[37]

At the MFGB Conference on 26 February, called to decide whether to accept the Commission, delegate after delegate spoke against. Even Robert Smillie, MFGB president, himself admitted —

much later: 'We had had many years' experience of Commissions — Commissions which had been appointed in the past in order to kill questions.'[38]

Yet it was Smillie himself, and Frank Hodges, secretary of the MFGB, both heroes of the left, who set about stamping out this opposition.

Lenin repeated hundreds of times that reforms are the by-product of revolutionary struggle: '. . . partial improvements can be (and always have been in history) merely a by-product of revolutionary class struggle.'[39] 'The truth that reforms are possible only as a by-product of a movement that is completely free of all narrowness of reformism has been confirmed a hundred times in world history.'[40]* Out of the semi-revolutionary situation of January to March 1919 came the sop of the Sankey Commission.

Smillie admitted later:

*This truth was hardly anywhere more strikingly illustrated than in the government's radical attitude to the acute housing problem. The housing campaign, Lloyd George told the Cabinet, would give the people a 'sense of confidence' in the *status quo* and prove that there was no need to resort to revolution in order to improve their lot. Compared to the enormous ends that the housing campaign would secure, cost was irrelevant: as the parliamentary secretary put it in April 1919, 'the money we are going to spend on housing is an insurance against Bolshevism and revolution' (**Hansard**, 8 April 1919).

Council housing rose from a mere 2 per cent of new houses built for the 15 years prior to 1914 to more than 60 per cent of new houses for the period between January 1919 and March 1923. And that was not all. These new houses were totally different to the long terraces of pre-war houses, surrounded by nothing but tarmac and brick. According to the government's Housing Manual of 1919, there were to be no more than 12 houses to the acre, with gardens, trees and open spaces, in the manner established by Raymond Unwin at Hampstead Garden Suburb. Inside they were to include features that previously had been found only in the houses of the middle classes.

When the revolutionary tide receded less than two years after the war, the campaign was brought to an abrupt close, both as regards the number of new houses built, and also their quality, which reverted to earlier standards of working-class housing (Mark Swenarton, 'An "Insurance against Revolution": Ideological Objectives of the Provision and Design of Public Housing in Britain after the First World War', **Bulletin of the Institute of Historical Research**, May 1981).

I have not the slightest doubt in my own mind that, if the miners were so advised, they could, within a month, stop every mine in the country till the mines are nationalised. That will stop all the railways and the other industries dependent upon coal.

But, faced with the most crucial choice anyone ever hand, 'We do not want to do that,' he said. 'We want to act "constitutionally", as it is called by the Government.'[41]

Frank Hodges later wrote in his autobiography that he and Robert Smillie 'threw in the whole weight of our argument and our influence to get the men and delegates to accept the Royal Commission. Hours, days, were spent in this tussle' including a national tour of the mining areas, 'and in the end we won'[42] — by a narrow majority.

This was a turning point in the whole industrial and political situation. At a peak of revolutionary potential, historical destiny may be embodied in one person. In Russia it was Lenin, leader of the Bolshevik Party, who steered history on to the side of the revolution and workers' power. In Britain it was the union official Robert Smillie who, though known as a left-winger, steered it on to the side of the capitalist class and mere reform.

Strike notices were not withdrawn. Their operation, scheduled for 15 March, was suspended for a fortnight to enable the initial report of the Sankey Commission to be scrutinised. The labour historian Allen Hutt describes the three weeks until the Commission's interim report came out on 20 March: 'The effect of the Commission's proceedings was sensational. Newspapers compared it with a revolutionary tribunal. Coal capitalism was in the dock — it seemed — on trial for its life.'[43]

The Interim Report dealt with the economic questions of wages and hours, leaving nationalisation for the final report in June. Although not conceding the miners' full demands, it offered significant reforms — an advance of two shillings (10p) a shift and a reduction of working hours from eight to seven per day. Taking the reduction in hours into account, the wage increase was in the region of 20 per cent. It also appeared to promise jam tomorrow, by stating that 'even upon the evidence already given, the present system of ownership and working in the coal industry stands condemned and some other system must be substituted for it . . . we are prepared to report now that it is in the interests of the country that the colliery workers shall in the future have an effective voice in the direction of the mines.'[44]

In addition, Bonar Law, on 20 March — the day the Interim Report came out — in the name of the Cabinet, repeated the assurances of the Report on control of the industry in the House of Commons,[45] and on the next day put in writing to the MFGB confirmation 'that the Government are prepared to carry out in the spirit and in the letter the recommendation of Sir John Sankey's Report.'

At precisely the same time as the government was selling Sankey for all it was worth, it was bending over backwards to buy off the railwaymen — whose dispute was at the same critical point — and divide them from the miners. The government delivered significant concessions there too; Jimmy Thomas worked overtime and the railway strike was called off.

At the same time as dangling the carrot, Bonar Law threatened to wield the big stick: if the miners struck, 'the government would use all the resources of the state without hesitation,'[46] as the prime minister had threatened in February. This was sheer bravado, as it would have been impossible for the government to deploy sufficient reliable troops to suppress by violence a strike movement that would have embraced the whole country. As for the police, 'it is feared that when disturbances occur reliance is not to be placed upon the police as a body,' reported Home Office spies.[47] There is nothing like fraternisation of troops and strikers (which happened even six months later in the railway strike) to raise the revolutionary élan which in the spring of 1919 ran so high.

The government had used every stratagem at its disposal, even to denunciation of its friends the coal-owners and their system. But, as J T Murphy incisively remarked of the Interim Report,

> this moral condemnation of the system did not worry the Government. They were more concerned about the mass

attack of the workers upon the system. The talking time of the Commission they regarded as profitable time, let the Commission say what they might. So long as the miners were kept at work each day was a gain to the Government and the mine-owners.[48]

For the second crucial time Smillie and Hodges bent all their efforts to getting the miners to accept the proposal. In view of the agitation against acceptance, the executive committee of the MFGB issued a manifesto to the miners on the evening of 27 March which ended with a strong appeal to continue working and to trust to the justice of their cause and the power of their organisation to attain their object.[49] Even so, a conference of the biggest federation, the South Wales Miners' Federation, voted on 31 March by 169 to 102 to advise its members to reject the government offer based on the Sankey Report,[50] a vote that materialised in 'large stoppages of work . . . in South Wales through the feeling engendered by the action of the National Executive.'[51] So Smillie and Hodges went on a second national tour of the coalfields to sell acceptance,[52] and by the time the ballot was held on 10 April they had decisively clinched the vote their way: 693,084 for, 76,992 against.

Later in the year Smillie spoke of their two fateful interventions, first to accept the Commission on 26-27 February, secondly to accept the Interim Report on 20 March:

Mr Hodges and myself were twice responsible during this discussion . . . for advising our men in the face of their ballot. We were prepared as a Federation, by a majority of ten to one, to carry on the strike for which the men had balloted, but Hodges and myself pleaded with our delegates to accept the Commission, and I think it only fair to say that the Miners' delegates showed considerable personal loyalty to us, in face of their ballot, by accepting the Commission. When the Commission gave their findings, our men were not satisfied. Their claims as to wages and hours were not fairly met. At their own conference, they rejected the official recommendation, and Hodges and myself urged that this was the finding of the Commission, and we advised them to accept it. They reluctantly accepted our advice.[53]

The government could smack its lips. Thomson's 'Fortnightly Report on Revolutionary Organisations in the UK and Morale Abroad' could report on 7 April: 'A comparatively peaceful fortnight is again to be recorded. The settlement with the "Triple Alliance", and particularly with the Coal Miners, has given general satisfaction.'[54]

The government had made an offer of the least it thought it could get away with to prevent a mass strike and challenge to the power of the state. The trade union officials then sold this to the workers.

A revolutionary peak is of short duration — at least the prime minister understood this, when he said on 24 February: 'for the prevention of civil strife . . . time is very essential . . . it is a matter of hours, let alone days'[55] — and the potential died as far as this crisis was concerned. J T Murphy cogently described the aftermath: the prevention of the strike 'transformed the demands of the miners for nationalisation of the mines and the democratic control of the industry into mere propaganda. Having done that, not all the subsequent campaigning of the Labour Party and the trade unions could re-transform these demands into issues which would secure mass action.'[56]

The government could breathe again. It had successfully ridden the crisis and passed the point of greatest danger.

The final report of the Sankey Commission came out on 23 June. Proposals for nationalisation and the granting to the miners of a share in control were common to the reports of the chairman and the six miners' spokesmen, which thus constituted in effect a Majority Report. Five of the employers' and coal owners' representatives opposed any change in ownership. The sixth, Sir Arthur Duckham, produced a scheme of his own for the trustification of the industry with elaborate district profit-pooling and regulating arrangements.

The government, from placation in its hour of need, now turned to provocation in its hour of triumph. Negotiations over piece-rate adjustments which followed the introduction of the seven-hour day were disrupted by the government's prohibition of any increase in excess of 10 per cent. This caused a bitter month-long strike of the 150,000 Yorkshire miners from mid-July to mid-August. Troops were sent and naval ratings put to man the pumps.[57] The miners won, but Lloyd George was able on 18 August, in the week the Yorkshire miners went back, to use the fact of the strike to justify breaking his earlier pledge to accept the Sankey Report 'in spirit and in letter' as the miners' leaders were now demanding, and instead opted for the Duckham alternative. Sankey's proposals for nationalisation, he said, were based

> entirely on the expectation that there will be increased har-mony between employer and worker in the mines. But since Mr Justice Sankey penned that report two or three things have happened which I think would have induced him to change his mind at the time . . . What is the theory of those who say that nationalisation will produce harmony? It is the theory that, while they would ask the worker to strike against the employer who is making a profit, he will not strike against the State, which has only the common interest of all to look after. But then there was the Yorkshire strike. The Yorkshire strike was a direct strike against the Government.[58]

When it came to it, the Duckham proposals passed into limbo very quickly.

The miners were outraged. One of the miners' MPs, Vernon Hartshorn, who was also an executive member of the MFGB, asked in the debate in the House of Commons on 18 August: 'Why was the Commission set up? Was it a huge game of bluff? Was it never intended that if the reports favoured nationalisation we were to get it? . . . That is the kind of question the miners of the country will ask, and they will say "we have been deceived, betrayed, duped".'[59]

On 3 September a miners' conference unanimously rejected the government proposals. So were they going finally to resort to the strike they had put aside so long while waiting upon the government? No, Lloyd George had been right about the timing, and the opportunity had passed when the miners were ready for such action. The same conference *unanimously* rejected strike action 'at this stage' or any call on the Triple Alliance. Instead they decided to put their case to the TUC Congress which met a few days later. Congress decided that the Parliamentary Committee of the TUC (it was later renamed the General Council) should intercede with the prime minister. The prime minister repeated his refusal of nationalisation on 9 October.

The final gasp was made at a special TUC Congress on 9-10 December 1919. Here, with no hope of a revival of the springtime fever, Smillie spoke bravely: 'The only thing that would move the Government is industrial force. We were given a Commission because the men had balloted on a strike. If the Government again refuse to carry out the findings of the Commission it will be the duty of the miners to tell them that action will be taken.'[60] But the delegates voted that the question should be put off till the spring of 1920, while a big educational campaign should be undertaken to rally public opinion.

This was called 'Mines for the Nation'. The campaign brought forth nearly a hundred demonstrations in cities and towns, many meetings, some attracting audiences of between 3,000 and 5,000, 15 million leaflets, and tens of thousands of pamphlets and articles in all trade union journals.[61] When all this public support, counted in millions, was distilled in terms of readiness for industrial action at the next Special TUC in March 1920, it amounted to a vote of one million for 'trade union action in the form of general strike' and nearly four million for 'political action in the form of intensive political propaganda in preparation for a General Election.'[62]

THE NATIONAL railway strike of 1919 followed closely the pattern of the miners' threatened strike for a key period of its lengthy maturation. The miners and railwaymen were two of the partners in the Triple Alliance which had agreed to act in solidarity; negotiations came to a head at the same time, the first three months of 1919; the state's forces of repression, the army and police, were too unreliable to have coped with a huge national strike of these two key sectors; the rank and file in both unions were straining at the leash, with numerous unofficial strikes breaking out in all quarters; and the union officials were being pushed much beyond their wishes, but moving on in order to keep control of their members, to keep the dispute purely industrial and within the bounds of trade union sectionalism.

There were differences, the main being that Jimmy Thomas, general secretary of the National Union of Railwaymen, was a well-known right-winger, while Smillie of the miners had the reputation of being a left-winger. These differences were exploited by Lloyd George to good effect. But the greater similarity superceded the differences: they both sold out their members simultaneously in one of the most far-reaching betrayals in British history — far-reaching because the unique concatenation of circumstances at the time meant the alternative could have been a workers' uprising.

Between the miners and the railwaymen, it was more urgent for the government to settle with the miners. First, the miners were by far the biggest union, a million strong; the railwaymen were half that.[1] Secondly, the railwaymen had already had something on account, namely, an eight-hour day, which started on 1 February; the miners hadn't. Thirdly, coal was the government's most pressing requirement.

So Lloyd George bent his efforts to dealing with the miners, which meant he had to somehow hold back the railway negotiations. Thomas was more than willing to oblige. For over half a year he and John Bromley, general secretary of the locomotivemen's union ASLEF, struggled to hold their rebellious members back from striking. The government meanwhile made its preparations, and it was only government provocation, when it was good and ready, that forced a strike on 26 September on the reluctant leaders, as the lesser evil to unofficial walk-outs.

Trouble had been brewing even before the implementation of the eight-hour day. Bromley sent a letter to the Cabinet on 17 January 1919: 'My Executive . . . have now passed a resolution to the effect that they view with grave concern the serious delay to the consideration of the Society's national wage programme, especially after your undertaking of December 16th that we should meet and go straight on with the negotiations.'

Management tried to claw back the eight-hour day. On the day of its implementation, 1 February, they posted up notices that the five-minute break at 6am and 10pm to enable men to wash their hands had been cancelled — after 40 years.[2] Meal times were cut out, a provocation which brought out the London tubes on 3 February for the best part of a week till they got satisfaction, over the heads of their leaders. The union leaders had urged them to return to work and signed an agreement the men refused to accept.

In addition to these affronts, the rest of the railwaymen's National Programme, in which the central demand was for an upward standardisation of wage rates for all grades, was the object of such deliberate delaying tactics that the men in the London and Liverpool districts insisted on calling a strike. Jimmy Thomas had considerable difficulty in stopping this; he held them back on the promise of discussions with the Railway Executive on 12 February[3]

56

— which was the date of the MFGB Conference which decided to ballot its members on strike action.

Meanwhile Thomas pleaded desperately with Lloyd George, outlining how serious it would be if he were forced to use his union's industrial strength:

> No-one can minimise the seriousness of that situation. I frankly recognise that the issue as it appears to me is this: if we have on the one hand a strike of these three great bodies, it will not only paralyse industry and may not only easily ruin the country, but even if we succeed by a strike, we shall have defeated the State, and that is, after all, a very serious thing which I do not minimise for a moment.[4]

On 25 February (the day the miners' huge majority in favour of strike was announced, and the Sankey Commission was offered) it was reported to the Cabinet that 'the two General Secretaries, Mr Thomas and Mr Bromley, had said they did not wish to present an ultimatum to the Government as the miners had done, but desired to arrive at an agreement by discussion.'[5]

At this historic turning point, Thomas and Smillie, the right and left-wing leaders of the two most powerful unions in the country, and of the all-powerful Triple Alliance, were burning the candle at both ends in order to sell out their respective members.

Lloyd George, meanwhile, was in Paris at the Peace Talks that followed the ending of the war. With Liverpool railwaymen reported seething with discontent and Birmingham ready to support the NUR Executive Committee in 'whatever action they deemed necessary', Thomas travelled to Paris to plead with Lloyd George for a few crumbs to take back, then came post-haste back to London on 19 March to take personal charge of developments.

This was the eve of the Sankey Commission's Interim Report, and one of the key moments in the calendar of the class struggle in Britain, the day a revolutionary party, had there been one, would have attempted to unite the rank-and-file miners, railwaymen and other workers who were straining at the leash, in an offensive general strike leading to a challenge for power.

Thomas lost not a moment in doing the opposite. The government, fully aware of the precipitous situation, held two Cabinet meetings on that day, 19 March. Sir Eric Geddes, minister of reconstruction and National Service, reported that 'Mr Thomas had said that if the men were treated reasonably, he would do his utmost to prevent a strike.' The minister of labour, perfectly in tune with Brother Thomas, said: 'it was worth while to pay the extra costs of the railwaymen's demands in order to secure their support at the present time.'[6]

So to avoid revolution, the Cabinet offered reforms: '. . . continuation of war wage plus wage till end of year; extra for night work; time and a half for Sunday duty and time and a quarter for overtime to be uniform on all lines; machinery in the new Ways and Means Communications Ministry by which the railwaymen should be permitted to make representations on questions of management.'[7] They had already won a shorter working week, a guaranteed day and week, a week's holiday after a year's service, and a recognition of the principle — not the implementation in hard cash, but a promise — of standardisation upwards, which was the main demand[8] — reforms all grudgingly conceded by the government to prevent a major challenge to their power.

(The Cabinet took the precaution meanwhile of advising all stationmasters that if they scabbed in a strike they would be given an additional seven days' leave as compensation.)[9]

Not yet aware of the Cabinet conclusions of the previous day, a Special General Meeting of the NUR on 20 March decided to ask the Triple Alliance to support them in calling a national strike. On 21 March (with Smillie now working at full pressure to kill opposition to the Sankey Commission's Interim Report), the Triple Alliance leaders — Thomas, Smillie, Williams — decided against an immediate strike: 'They thought it better to see if the Government would concede to the Alliance what it would not to the railwaymen alone. They advised the members of the NUR to continue at work and await the outcome of the new discussions.'[10]

The 'outcome of the new discussions' was disclosed to the railwaymen by Bonar Law, deputising for Lloyd George while he was in Paris. Although the main issue of standardisation upwards was conceded in principle only — and we know the emptiness of such pledges by the government — the strike was called off on 27 March. The miners accepted the Sankey Interim Report soon afterwards.

The crisis was over. The revolutionary situation had passed.

The workers' struggles, however, still went on. A general feeling of unrest was widespread throughout the working class during the summer months of July and August, and rank-and-file militancy boiled over on several occasions. In April 15,000 Mersey dockers struck over stopping and starting times. The biggest strike of the year started on 23 June, when 450,000 cotton workers struck work for 18 days, forcing a reduction in the working week from 55½ hours to 48, and a wage increase of 30 per cent.[11] A miners' strike was provoked in July in Yorkshire when the Coal Controllers revised a previous decision and forbade a rise in piecework rates that had been agreed between the Yorkshire Miners' Association and the Yorkshire Employers' Association. 150,000 Yorkshire miners came out and sections of other coalfields — in Scotland, Kent, Leicestershire and South Wales — struck work over similar disputes. The police struck at the end of July for union recognition. Railwaymen on the North Eastern Railway stopped work in July over the suspension of ten men, and for a short time the rank and file and their strike committee ignored the negotiations of the NUR Executive.[12]

It was clear to the government that its concessionary policy in the hour of its greatest need had not dealt a mortal blow to the beast of working-class unrest. The government needed, then, to prepare its defence and offence, and provoke the showdown when it felt it could handle it. The yet unresolved railway dispute was to provide the opportunity. Through this showdown the government hoped to turn the tide and implement 'the universal determination of the capitalists to reduce wages to pre-war level.'[13]

By August the government felt it was gaining control. The strike of Yorkshire miners had been settled by a compromise accepted in all the coalfields. On the law-and-order side demobilisation was working more smoothly and the police strike had been smashed. Lloyd George threw out the Sankey Commission recommendation to nationalise the mines on 18 August and there were no repercussions.

The railway dispute was now clearly coming to a head. In June the NUR and ASLEF presented a united claim on the question of the pay of footplatemen — since both unions numbered footplatemen among their members. As the government had hitherto succeeded so splendidly with a divide-and-rule policy, it settled the claim of these top-grade men on 20 August at the highest rate of pay pertaining to footplatemen, up from £3 18s to £4 10s, an increase of 13.3 per cent.[14] This was 'a charter of service unparalleled in the history of British locomotivemen,' according to a historian of ASLEF.[15]

But as a result the movement for standardisation upwards of the wage rates of all other grades — porters, guards, shunters, etc. — grew in intensity throughout August and early September.[16]

The government now felt confident that the time was ripe for the showdown — even if the Triple Alliance partners acted in solidarity and the strike became a general strike. For by the latter part of the year the Triple Alliance's edge was blunted. As labour historian Alastair Hatchett writes:

> The formation and existence of the Alliance reflected the militancy of rank and file pressure for a General Staff for Labour, and as such it was a product of the mainstream of syndicalist thought; yet paradoxically it was this pressure that moulded the official conception of it and the motive for establishing it. It was certainly not the intention of the moderate leaders like J H Thomas, or the reactionary Havelock Wilson, to intensify the class struggle. They supported the new formation in the hope that sympathetic and local strikes might be reduced to a minimum, and to reinforce the authority of their leadership. Robert Smillie argued against the misconceived idea that a strike by any section of the miners, railwaymen or transport workers would be given the general backing of the Alliance. Thus it was that the most important

60

industrial organisation of the post-war period was founded, not as a spearhead for a new phase of struggle, but as a defensive measure of a hard-pressed union leadership.[17]

The Triple Alliance's record gave the government confidence that it need not fear too much. On 21 March 1919 the Alliance had refused the NUR Special General Meeting's request for a national strike. On 23 July the NUR delegation to an Alliance conference advocated strike action to compel the government to abolish conscription, pull out of Russia, and stop military intervention in industrial disputes. This was turned down in favour of a membership ballot by the separate Alliance unions. On 4 September the Alliance then decided to postpone this membership ballot indefinitely.[18]

The government felt it could take the risk and girded its loins. It appointed the Geddes brothers, Eric (now minister of transport and government troubleshooter) and Auckland, president of the Board of Trade, to handle negotiations.

At the beginning of September General Haig, Commander-in-Chief, called a high-level meeting of the seven generals of the army home commands 'to discuss our plans for dealing with a General Strike.' These were 'very complete' and the generals assured Haig that their plans were 'quite ready to put into force at any moment.'[19]

The government offer was put to the railwaymen on 19 September. If the provocation was to work, it had to be strong enough to override Jimmy Thomas's infinite opposition to strike action. And it was. Far from 'standardisation upwards', the government demanded draconian wage cuts of between one and sixteen shillings (5p and 80p) a week, with a basic wage in the lowest grade of only 40s (£2) a week. 100,000 men would have their pay cut; no one would get more. The offer, 'definite' in its first draft, was changed to 'definitive' by Sir Auckland Geddes, thus becoming an ultimatum.[20]

Aghast, the NUR executive met on 24 September, a Wednesday, and sent instructions to all branches to strike at midnight on Friday 27 September. Still the indefatigable Thomas continued to plead with ministers and the prime minister on 24 and 25 September,[21] assuring them that the union was ready to cancel the strike notices immediately 'if the answer of the Cabinet is such that would warrant that step.'[22]

The government meanwhile replaced the Industrial Unrest Committee with a stronger Strike Committee, with extensive executive powers and Eric Geddes in the chair. Its main task was the maintenance of food supplies and 'protection'.[23] This was the forerunner of the better-known Supply and Transport Organisation, which was to figure so prominently in the 1926 General Strike. The government had previously taken the precaution of keeping control of sugar, wheat and other foodstuffs while de-controlling all else, in readiness for a showdown with the unions.[24] It had kept army units which should have reverted to peace-time activities in reserve for strike-breaking purposes, and now got ready to deploy 23,000 troops from these units on 'protection' duties, holding 30,000 in reserve. It also spoke of forming companies of Special Constables to relieve the army.

Eric Geddes continued the line of provocation well into the strike, announcing on 3 October that wages earned in the week up to the start of the strike on 26 September would be withheld.[25] The government also undertook an intensive press campaign with a daily bulletin supplied to all newspapers from Downing Street under the personal direction of Sir William Sutherland, one of the prime minister's private secretaries.[26] The prime minister denounced the strike as an 'anarchist conspiracy', 'a wanton attempt to hold up the community'. Poor respectable Jimmy Thomas, MP and Privy Councillor!

This time the cards were all stacked in the government's favour, and it seemed that it could not fail to win. Yet it didn't win. This was by and large because the rank and file of workers were not yet quiescent, and came, or tried to come, to the assistance of the railwaymen.

The strike was rock solid among NUR men. The government's divide-and-rule tactic with the higher-grade ASLEF workers misfired, as 57,000 members, spurning the August bribe, came out in solidarity from day one till the settlement nine days later on 5 October. The government had also misjudged the reliability of the troops, for some fraternised with the pickets and had to be promptly withdrawn to barracks, 'and the Cabinet was warned, by high military authority, against attempting to use the troops.'[27]

There were demands from London busmen, tramway workers and dockers to the Transport Workers' Federation to call its members out on strike,[28] and compositors and machine men on the London newspapers threatened to down tools unless the papers gave the railwaymen's case a fair show.[29] The Co-operative Wholesale movement rose magnificently to the occasion, making emergency arrangements to hand over £500,000 which the unions needed for strike pay, and accepting vouchers from strike committees in exchange for food.[30]

It should be noted, however, that the transport workers sought official sanction for strike action and stayed at work when this was not forthcoming. In the early part of the year the more usual practice had been an unofficial walk-out.

Thomas and other trade union leaders did their best to damp down the enthusiasm. Thomas admitted that he was conducting the strike himself, because he knew the dangers of a revolution.[31] He kept the Triple Alliance strictly out of negotiations, not even informing them of progress, so that, as Robert Williams of the Transport Workers' Federation complained, the first the Alliance heard about the negotiations was 'what they learned in the newspapers'. This was after the NUR Executive committee had specifically instructed Thomas on 25 September to notify the Triple Alliance of the position.[32]

Thomas and the NUR executive committee declined the numerous offers of sympathetic strike action.[33] His chief endeavour was to cramp the potential of the strike, and keep it as an economic issue, away from politics. From the beginning, he told the final rally of railwaymen on 5 October, he was 'determined to make the issue a wage question and nothing more'. He was afraid that if the railwaymen called for the assistance of other unions a dispute which began on the question of railway wages might end by having political and constitutional implications — a development to which he was strenuously opposed.[34]

The enthusiasm of the transport workers to support their railway comrades found disfavour in the eyes of at least some of *their* leaders too. Ernest Bevin, then a dockers' leader, was afraid, if the strike continued, of the railway unions 'stumbling into an ineffectual challenge to the power of the state.' On 1 October he got a conference called of unions affected, set up a mediation committee to help carry negotiations through, and sent a deputation to the prime minister, but found that he was still thinking in terms of railway surrender — not negotiations. So the mediation committee pressed more urgently, sending a further message to the prime minister that unless 'a more reasonable attitude' was adopted by his Cabinet, 'it would be impossible to avert a widespread extension of the strike with all its consequences'. The government got the message; it gave way.[35]

The 'definitive' offer was explained away. By the settlement of 5 October, there were to be no cuts. Existing rates were stabilised (and the lowest grade even secured an increase in basic rate). Full reinstatement and no victimisation was unconditionally conceded; and the impounded week's arrears of pay was paid. The strike saved the railwaymen's pay and conditions and those of the rest of the working class for well over a year.[36]

The strike provided another opportunity, even if not so ripe as in the spring, to broaden the struggle and challenge the state. The workers' militancy had not yet been quenched; their readiness to fight for their class had once more shown itself. The opportunity was lost because Thomas and other union leaders took pains to prevent any such eventuality. 'We did not want to beat the government,' said Thomas at the final rally in the Albert Hall on 5 October.[37] Only a well-rooted revolutionary party, conscious of its aims, could have led the workers forward.

THE GOVERNMENT'S handling of these major crises — iron fist for Glasgow, kid gloves for the miners and railwaymen — showed the height of refinement the British ruling class reached after centuries of experience in suppressing its wage slaves. It understood not only the objective material circumstances, but also the subjective consciousness of the *dramatis personae* — the social role and psychology of the trade union officials, the temper of the rank and file and the parameters of the movement.

Take the objective circumstances first. The hunger for armaments abated with the end of the war. The engineers — the Clyde in general — was therefore less indispensible. But the mines and railways *were* indispensible, after the war as much as during it, since they underpinned the whole economy. Coal stocks were critically low, and every nugget of coal cut was snapped up. The government could therefore afford to spurn the engineers, but not the miners and railwaymen.

Another determining issue was the localisation of the engineers compared with the national threat of the miners. We have seen how the leadership of the Glasgow strike failed to extend the strike much beyond the Clydeside engineers. Glasgow could therefore be isolated. A miners' strike, on the other hand, had national connotations from the start, and there was always the possibility that the Jimmy Thomases of the Triple Alliance might be forced by a rebellious rank and file to support the miners — he made the threat often enough. Once again the government could spurn the engineers, but not the miners and railwaymen.

But the key factor determining the government's strategy lay, as always, in the subjective factor, the relationship with the trade union bureaucracies. 'The government's policy was to stand by the trade unions and support their executive authority,' proclaimed the minister of labour.[1]

The ASE leaders were out-and-out right-wingers, and their animosity to their unofficial counterpart, the Clyde Workers Committee, was fierce. They opposed the Glasgow strike tooth and nail, and when the workers took no notice, they turned to the minister of labour for support. The government decided 'it could not actively' — for 'actively' read 'openly' — 'interfere in the settlement of these strikes over the heads of the Union Executives.'[2] This was stated at the Cabinet meeting of 28 January. The major events of the strike followed: Bloody Friday on 31 January was engineered by the government, and the suspension of the entire Glasgow, Belfast and London district committees of the union was carried out by the ASE executive on 6 February.

The miners' leaders were known as left-wingers. Robert Williams, leader of the Transport Workers and one of the best-known leading left-wingers among trade unionists, exclaimed: 'What working class leader could be more indicative of the spirit of proletarian revolt than Smillie?'[3] And from the right of the movement comes this affirmation: 'Everyone knows that there are today two outstanding figures in our trade union movement . . . Mr Robert Smillie and Mr Robert Williams. Their idea of industrial action is to create a revolution in this country and their idea of government is the Soviet Government of Russia.'[4] Frank Hodges began his career as a syndicalist in the South Wales Unofficial Reform Committee.[5] The congruence of pit, lodge and community produced a far closer relationship between the rank and file and officials of the Miners Federation than was the case with the engineers.

In these circumstances the government could smash the Clyde workers with the blessing of the engineers' official leaders. But they had to proceed by stealth and with utmost caution to win over the miners' leaders, who had to be persuaded on two counts: that the government's word was its bond, however hollow the pledge; and that what was on offer was better for the workers than the alternative of government violence, vain though the threat may have been.

The strategy achieved 100 per cent success. On the first count, Smillie himself proclaimed to the TUC: 'We believed the government would carry out what we thought was its pledge to us.'[6] And on the second, he exclaimed: '. . . if there is a strike they will use the soldiers. My people will be shot down. Anything rather than that!'[7]

The prime minister was single-minded and imposed his will on the Cabinet team. His opposition in the trade union leadership was completely disunited, and he knew it. The First Lord of the Admiralty could aptly comment: 'When Labour representatives met together in the same room they were all suspicious of each other, and it rarely happened that they produced any useful proposals.'[8] Robert Williams showed some foresight when he said: 'I can clearly see that in formulating our various demands separately and distinctly . . . we shall be taken in detail and smashed separately.'[9]

How true this proved to be.

In the circumstances the prime minister was ready to twist and turn in any direction to disorient his disunited opposition, as was commented on in the presidential speech at the TUC: 'the prime minister, to tide over a temporary difficulty, will make any promise, with no intention of carrying it out — careless of what may happen in the future to his country or to his reputation.'[10]

Lloyd George and his Cabinet made love to the trade union and Labour Party bureaucracy when it suited them, and the Cabinet papers are full of their need for and appreciation of this liaison. Churchill conceded that the Triple Alliance strike threatened in February 'was averted by the good sense of all concerned, and notably by the assistance rendered by many Honourable Gentlemen sitting on the benches immediately opposite.'[11] Home secretary Shortt was even more effusive: 'I should like to take this opportunity of expressing the very strong appreciation held by the government of the action of all the really responsible leaders of Labour in these very troublesome times. There is no question about the patriotism and loyalty they have shown.'[12]

The home secretary turned Jimmy Thomas's sentiments to excellent effect. He repeats what Thomas said and comments:

> 'Unless you give way upon this etc. . . . there will be a strike.' And he went on to say, 'If we, the strikers, win, we have defeated the country.' That was a very, very important declaration to make, because it is perfectly clear that if a winning strike is a defeat of the country, a strike at all is an attack upon the country; and, therefore, it is perfectly clear . . . what the duty of the Government is in this matter. He has shown perfectly clearly that the Government now is put by him and his friends in the position of defending the country as a whole from attack by a small part of the community.[13]

Indeed, as Churchill said: 'The curse of Trade Unionism was that there was not enough of it, and it was not highly enough developed to make its branch secretaries fall into line with the head office.' Bonar Law 'thought that the Trade Union organisation was the only thing between us and anarchy, and if the Trade Union organisation was against us the position would be hopeless.'[14]

The minister of labour said: 'The goverment has the strongest interest in encouraging efficient trade union machinery.' Again, Bonar Law said the government must not intervene in local disputes, as this 'could only undermine the authority of those who have been chosen by the men to represent them, and would destroy the co-operation between employers and employed on which the hope of industrial peace depends.'[15]

The message may not reach home. It needs the mediation of friends closer to the workers whom they must control. One of the causes of industrial unrest, the prime minister maintained,

> is the sedulous attempt which had been made for years to undermine confidence in trade union leadership. That has produced indiscipline which has often been beyond the control of the trade unions. It has almost made collective bar-

gaining impossible, and I cannot conceive anything more fatal to the industrial life of this country . . . Knowledge and experience give responsibility, and the moment the leaders exercise that responsibility they are attacked. Their influence is undermined.

Lloyd George was just as ready to jilt his partner when he got no more satisfaction out of the embrace. The **Herald** noted the friendliness and solicitude of the government for official trade unionism in times of acute unrest — a feeling which sank into oblivion the moment order was restored.[16] By 18 August this was the case, and Lloyd George snubbed not only the miners by throwing out nationalisation, but even the faithful Jimmy Thomas: 'My right honourable Friend (Mr Thomas) has given us just as much trouble as my right honourable Friend (Mr Brace, Miners' MP) sitting on the same bench. I cannot distinguish between them — demands for higher wages, demands about hours, and so on . . .'[17]

THE TASK of the trade unions is to improve the terms on which workers are exploited *within* the capitalist system, not to end exploitation. While uniting the workers in one trade, as the name 'trade union' implies, they separate them from workers in other unions through the different wages, conditions and traditions pertaining in the different industries. As Cliff and Gluckstein state: 'The geography of trade unionism matches the geography of capitalism.'[1]

This sectionalism inevitably produces the trade union bureaucracy, whose special task is to carry out the union's function. This involves mediating between the employers and the workers, a job quite different to that of the workers they represent, be they engineers, miners, railwaymen, cleaners, teachers, office workers or whatever. Their role safeguards them from the job insecurity, the low wages, the constant conflicts with management faced by those they represent. Instead their role closets the union officials with management in endless hours of negotiation, whose very core is reconciliation between capital and labour, and whose expression is always compromise. They become a distinct, basically conservative, social stratum.

To do their specific bureaucratic job effectively the officials must always maintain as tight a control of their members as possible. This requires them to balance between different sections of the membership. They need to hold back the militants — particularly the political ones whose ideas transcend the purely economic issues of a dispute — and keep the members as passive as possible.

There may, however, be occasions when the bureaucracy are dragged or provoked into a strike; then they may need to urge the apathetic members to make some minimal show of combativity to prevent the union, and with it the bureaucrats, being pushed right back into ignominious defeat. Since the officials will avoid strikes as long as they can, their overriding activity is the subordination of the active vanguard among workers rather than the encouragement of the passive rearguard — though the latter may figure more prominently in the pronouncements of the bureaucrats as an alibi for their own unwillingness to fight.

The fear of losing control of the members is the perpetual nightmare of the bureaucracy, threatening their very *raison d'être*. In the 1919 Labour Party Conference debate on striking as a means of political action, James Sexton, leader of the dock labourers (and an MP), said of its advocates that

> . . . they were letting loose an element that was rife to-day in the Trade Union Movement, that would take every advantage of the confusion, and make it impossible for them to exercise any controlling power . . . They were letting loose an element they could not control. They had no machinery to replace what they destroyed. Their only machinery would be revolution. It was all very well to talk about revolution. He was a revolutionist of a social character, and believed in social revolution(!). But he did not believe in letting mad dogs loose, and that was what they were asking for. They would be destroying their organisation, destroying their Movement. By a strike as a means of political action, they would be going in a direction which would bring a big risk of breaking up their organisation, letting loose forces they could not control, and asking for civil war in this country.[2]

Within the bureaucracy there are differences between individual officials. Differences between the unions in conditions and traditions, class pressures from below and above, the officials' own origins, push them to the right or the left. In particular, the rise to office of many through the ranks as outstanding fighters for their class lives on as reputation long after the fight has become mere rhetoric. This is, on the one hand, a useful lever of control for the official, but on the other it can open up opportunities for the rank and file to split the bureaucracy and weaken its conservative hold. In general, the greater the bureaucrat's distance in time from the workplace, the more conservative and right wing he or she is. A catalogue of the political development of officials who sounded revolutionary in 1919 is tragic testimony to this.

Robert Williams, leader of the transport workers' union and hence of the Triple Alliance, and the most revolutionary of the officials, became a founding member of the Communist Party in June 1920. On Black Friday, 15 April 1921, with the other partner in the Triple Alliance, the railway workers, he failed to come to the assistance of the miners — who were left to fight alone for three months. For this sell-out he was expelled from the Communist Party. He turned towards the Labour Party, becoming its chairman for 1925-6, the year of the General Strike, when the miners were again sold out. He ended up supporting Ramsay MacDonald in the Tory-controlled National Government of 1931.

Frank Hodges started his career as a militant syndicalist in the miners' Unofficial Reform Committee in South Wales. The higher he climbed in the union apparatus the more right-wing he became. He gave up the secretaryship of the MFGB when he became Civil Lord of the Admiralty in the Labour government of 1924. He ended his days as a mine-*owner* and director of a number of companies.

Jimmy Thomas, on the other hand, was always a right-winger, and it is not surprising he too ended up in Ramsay MacDonald's Tory-controlled National Government.[3]

Robert Smillie was always a parliamentarian, even at the height of the industrial struggle. His reaction to Churchill's Secret Circular was: 'The document seems to have been issued in connection with the recent strike threat by the Triple Alliance. The moral is that people should vote the right way when they next have the chance.'[4] Smillie's total lack of any theoretical principle enabled him to second the following racist resolution, which was carried at the 1919 TUC: 'That immediate steps be taken to abolish all underpaid Asiatic labour in the merchant marine, and that preference of employment be given first to British whites, and secondly to British coloureds, rather than Chinamen.'[5]

As Cliff and Gluckstein state:

> The *fundamental* fact . . . overriding all differences between bureaucrats, is that they belong to a conservative social stratum, which, especially at times of radical crisis — as in the 1926 General Strike — makes the differences between left and right-wing bureaucrats *secondary*. At such times *all* sections of the bureaucracy seek to curb and control workers' militancy.[6]

Lloyd George, well-briefed and wily, with a total view of the class struggle, knew how to exploit the disunity of the workers — the sectionalism of the trade unions, the differences between right and left-wing bureaucrats on the one hand, and the differences between the bureaucrats as a whole and the rank-and-file membership of their unions on the other — with the aim of getting them, whatever their political stance, to sell their members out.

Lloyd George succeeded brilliantly in achieving this for his class, the ruling class.

To prevent workers going beyond economic struggles and challenging the government, the ruling class presents the state as a neutral institution, above classes, serving the best interests of 'the community', 'the nation', 'the country'. Its overthrow could produce only 'anarchy', 'Bolshevism', 'tyranny'.

The prevailing ideas in society, as Marx stated, are the ideas of the ruling class, and it is only when working-class struggle rises to revolutionary proportions, and workers gain confidence in their own ability to emancipate themselves, that they throw off the shackles of bourgeois ideology, see the state as it is: the instrument of the rule of one class over others, and are prepared to smash it in order to achieve their own emancipation.

But the emancipation of the working class is not exactly what the trade union bureaucrats want. Indeed, it would eliminate their specific role and their status, which capitalism preserves. They therefore completely embrace the bourgeois ideology of the state, and speak in almost identical terms as the government. It is thus in the trade union bureaucrats that the government finds its vehicle for communicating with the workers, especially in times of working-class upsurge.

Lloyd George had an interview with the leaders of the Triple Alliance early in 1919, during which he said:

> Gentlemen, you have fashioned, in the Triple Alliance of the unions represented by you, a most powerful instrument. I feel bound to tell you that in our opinion we are at your mercy. The Army is disaffected and cannot be relied upon. Trouble has occurred already in a number of camps. We have just emerged from a great war and the people are eager for the reward of their sacrifice, and we are in no position to satisfy them. In these circumstances, if you carry out your threat and strike, then you will defeat us.
>
> But if you do so, have you weighed the consequences? The strike will be in defiance of the Government of this country and by its very success will precipitate a constitutional crisis of the first importance. For, if a force arises in the State which is stronger than the State itself, then it must be ready to take on the functions of the State itself, or withdraw and accept the authority of the State. Gentlemen, have you considered, and if you have, are you ready?

'From that moment on,' said Robert Smillie, 'we were beaten and we knew we were.'[7]

Lloyd George sensed better than anyone how to touch the vital nerve. Prey to anxiety, in the period of Britain's greatest revolutionary potential, February 1919, he pleads with the miners through patriotism:

> The country will gain nothing by purchasing temporary immunity by giving way . . . I beg them (the miners) above all, when this country has through its sacrifice won such a

position in the world, not to destroy its influence, not to destroy its power, not to destroy its prosperity and not to precipitate it into a great disaster.[8]

Then the appeal to the state, whose sanctity prevails over all. The attempt to undermine trade union officials

is done undoubtedly by some for the very reason that anarchy is the only thing that can follow, and that is what they are after. Anarchy is their aim, and anarchy is the purpose of some of these men who are seeking to destroy not merely trade unionism, but the State.[9]

The prime minister found the echo he needed in Jimmy Thomas, who said, two days later:

I have no hesitation in saying, with a full sense of responsibility, that, serious as has been the industrial trouble in the past, the difficulty with the miners, the railwaymen, and the transport workers at this moment is so serious that this country may be plunged at any moment in one of the greatest industrial upheavals that it has ever known . . .

But, he goes on,

. . . however strong the trade union movement may be — and it is strong — however powerful the trade union movement is — and it is powerful — it is not stronger, more powerful or more important than the State as a whole. In other words, whilst we must be prepared to fight and defend our rights as trade unionists and workers, we can only defend those rights when they are consistent with, and in harmony with, our position as citizens of the State as a whole.[10]

At the same session of the House of Commons, William Brace, Labour MP and national executive member of the MFGB, pressed the point home, at the same time vividly exposing the bureaucratic view of the nationalisation of the mines:

To appeal to workmen in the name of the State is to touch them in their most vital spot, their native patriotism. If you would allow us to appeal to the workmen to withhold doing anything in the form of the industrial action policy because it was the property of the State and on behalf of the State, we should be able to be infinitely more effective than any appeal that can be made to them if the concerns are to be allowed to continue in the hands of and under the control of private individuals.[11]

For the rank-and-file miners who balloted by a majority of six-to-one for strike action at the time, nationalisation was a vision with revolutionary implications, promising an end to grinding poverty, abominable housing, and in particular the disastrous death toll caused by callous, profiteering private coal-owners (1,451 killed according to the most recent report at the time, on which the Inspector of Mines commented: 'The year was happily marked by the absence of any great disaster.')[12] Unfortunately there was no revolutionary party to encapsulate their dream and lead the fight to realise it. For the leadership that did exist, the trade union and Labour Party bureaucracy, the ballot result and strike threat only showed 'how near the country is to disaster', as Adamson, leader of the Parliamentary Labour Party and of the Fife Miners' Federation,[13] put it.

J R Clynes, a prominent Labour MP, who was later to become leader of the party, said in the debate on 11 February 1919, after the prime minister had threatened the miners:

> I think the whole of my Honourable Friends are in agreement . . . with the Prime Minister when he said that disorder must be put down, that such acts of crime as in a few instances have been committed, such excesses as I say without hesitation have now and then disgraced the record of labour, must be resisted. With all that side of his case we are in the fullest agreement.

He then explains why such a stand is necessary:

> I stand not only for respect for the law, because we make it, but because some day those of us who have now to play the part of critic and sometimes of opponent of the Government may for aught we know be called upon by the country to be responsible for the making and administration of the law. We, or those who are to follow us, who may have that responsibility, should be careful of the examples which in

these days of less responsibility and greater freedom we may now set.

The workers' organisations must therefore bend all efforts to achieving this end:

> I want to see discipline maintained in these great organisations (trade unions). Some of these trade unions and their officers are now on their trial. I would ask these officers . . . not to surrender their self-respect to any degree of pressure that may be used against them in connection with any one of these industrial disputes.

And success has to be ensured by the right attitude of class collaboration at the point of production. He goes on: 'I want to see . . . in the workshop committees of men who will act not in any frame of mind of revolt against the firm or the heads of it . . .'[14]

Clynes was a most eloquent spokesman of the reformist viewpoint for the Labour party, as Jimmy Thomas was for the trade unions.

It was perfectly natural that these Labour leaders should be completely unembarrassed by the setting up in February 1919 of the government spy network to report on 'why there was so much revolt against the authority of the trade unions'. Clynes himself, on behalf of the Labour Party, was specially approached by the Home Office, and spoke in favour. When the capitalist class is pushed to the wall the reformists show their true colours most clearly.

WHAT THE government knew after the events it could not know before. The fire might have been doused in the spring of 1919, but who could say that the embers might not flare up again, as indeed they did in the railway strike later that same year. The strikes did not go away after the spring, but rumbled on at a high level throughout the year. So the government took precautionary measures on all fronts.

One of these measures was to get the workers drunk. When sobriety was needed for the war effort, the government had put strict controls on the quantity and quality of beer, with dramatic results in the decline of drinking offences.

With the post-war unrest, it set out to lift these controls and provide a narcotic to help still the ferment. An enormous amount of Cabinet time during the first six months of the year was taken up with one single item — beer, whose scarcity and 'washy' quality were rationalised as being a major cause of labour unrest. Indeed, at one entire Cabinet meeting on 23 June, the day the 450,000-strong cotton workers' strike began, beer was the only item on the agenda.[1]

At the Cabinet meeting of 24 January 1919, Bonar Law said: 'There was no doubt that many people attributed the present industrial unrest to the lack and poor quality of beer.' Sir Robert Horne attributed 'a good deal of irritation on the Clyde . . . to the lack of beer and the bad quality of that obtainable.' Whereupon the Food Controller suggested that 'a substantial reduction in the price and an increase in the supply would have a good effect on public opinion, and do much to allay the prevailing industrial unrest.' Thereupon it was agreed to increase the supply and quality and reduce the price of beer.[2]

On 13 March the First Lord of the Admiralty said that 'the working man regarded the indifferent quality of beer as a typical case of class legislation.'[3]

Even the advocates of temperance preferred beer to class struggle. The Food Controller reported that 'a temperance advocate had stated that unless more beer were available it would be difficult to keep people at work. Already there were reports of disturbances in the Provinces.'[4]

The Labour Party's view was no different. Bonar Law stated that 'representatives of the Labour Party, on whose opinion he placed great weight, advised him that hostility to the Government "was on account of the shortage and bad quality of beer," and that to give up restrictions on beer "would have the important effect of preventing agitation against the Budget . . ." Such an agitation would be very dangerous, and would spread all over the country, working upon the general discontent.'[5] This line of reasoning was repeated time and again.

Lack of beer led to early closing of pubs, a serious handicap to the government, as pubs 'have acted as meeting places where the men could discuss politics and "blow off steam".'[6]

As summer approached the Cabinet received alarmist reports of threatened strikes unless something was done. One Alderman Leese, a local magistrate, said in early June that he would be prepared to support a 'down tools' policy unless the Liquor Control Board was abolished.[7]

On 23 June the government removed all restrictions on quantity and allowed a much-improved quality of beer.

Compare this with the attitude of the Bolsheviks who, in the first days after the October 1917 revolution in Russia, smashed the vodka barrels and poured the liquor into the gutter, so that the workers should soberly carry forward the revolution and not be destroyed in a drunken stupor.

9

THE REVOLUTIONARY SITUATION of 1919 was essentially over by the end of March, with the government having the upper hand. By the latter part of the year, the previous bogey of the Triple Alliance had become rather an object of ridicule. The minister of labour pointed out that 'although they had expressed rather extreme views with regard to political action by industrial pressure, they had so far done little more than talk.'[1] Winston Churchill was reported as saying that 'if the Triple Alliance does not get a move on they will have some difficulty in having to make new grievances for the government to be approached on with a view to taking action.'[2]

Some in the trade union movement were irked. At the TUC in September a delegate from the union of stewards on board ship said:

I do not want this Congress to place itself in the position that the Triple Alliance has been placed in the last few weeks. On one occasion they took a vote in favour of direct action by an overwhelming majority but, instead of acting upon it, they held another meeting and confirmed their previous decision, and then they held a third meeting and confirmed it again. Personally, I take action to mean — direct action. If you are going to do it, do it, and don't talk so much about it. All they have been doing so far has been to talk and vote about it.[3]

To hide their betrayal and continue to pose as the militant leaders of the working class, the left-wing trade union leaders then indulged in a campaign of bellicose rhetoric around the issue of 'direct action' — in other words, industrial action for political purposes. The Labour Party conference held at Southport on 25-27 June 1919, and the TUC Congress held in Glasgow on 8-13 September, both resounded with the heat of lengthy argument between those who supported direct action — including Smillie and Hodges of the Miners' Federation and Robert Williams of the Transport Workers — and those who opposed it — including Jimmy Thomas, Clynes and the rest of the Labour MPs.

It is interesting to see how the campaign was started, as this gives a clue to its nature. The result of Smillie's and Hodges' successful efforts to sell the Sankey Interim Report was announced at an MFGB conference on 16 April, in the morning session. With lightning rapidity the retreat on industrial action at home turned into a rhetorical offensive on foreign affairs. With only the lunch break between them, the afternoon session passed a resolution demanding the abandonment of conscription and the withdrawal of troops from Russia, the raising of the blockade on Germany and the release of conscientious objectors. No action was decided by the miners' conference; instead the resolution was submitted to the Triple Alliance meeting to be held that same evening — with the rationale that it would have greater impact coming from the Alliance. No action was decided by the Triple Alliance; instead the resolution was submitted to the Parliamentary Committee of the TUC — with the rationale that *this* would have even greater impact. They were asked to convene a special national conference of the trade union movement where finally a decision should be taken as to what action, if any, should be taken to compel the government to comply with the terms of the resolution.[4] There was no less militant body, more removed from the workplace, that the Parliamentary Committee could pass the buck to, so instead it sent a deputation to see Bonar law, whose reply they found so satisfactory that they did not call a conference.

This gave scope for dramatic reprimands of the Parliamentary Committee by the left officials at the TUC, with Smillie leading the way. Words were not minced; sparks flew. '. . . there were members sitting on the Parliamentary Committee of the TUC who were more reactionary than the British Government,' exclaimed Robert Williams, as blast and counterblast heated the air of conference. The left won the day over the Parliamentary Committee, and it was instructed to call a Special Congress.[5]

At the beginning of the year the MFGB had not waited upon others to take decisions. Nor did the Triple Alliance. Certainly they did not involve the effete Parliamentary Committee. But then the rank and file were active, and pushing the officials forward. Now the officials were at the helm, and pressure from the rank and file absent. That made a strike out of the question. If they fought to prevent action over industrial issues, they were certainly not going to initiate action over political ones, despite all their hot protestations to the contrary. A Special TUC Congress was finally called in early December. It decided on the 'Mines for the Nation' campaign described above.

Thus 1919 ended with two campaigns, 'Mines for the Nation' and 'Direct Action' — both hot air balloons.

IO

THERE IS one permanent feature of the British scene that has hardly been mentioned. That is the Labour Party. The omission is not accidental. Whenever there was an industrial upsurge, the Labour Party was not to be seen. Rank-and-file Labour Party members were always active, but not the party as such. When the movement was defeated, or gains clawed back, Labour Party fortunes rose. The Labour Party has always been parasitic on the rise and defeat of industrial struggle.

The 1889 upsurge connected with the growth of New Unionism declined sharply after the employers' offensive of 1891-3; in 1893 the ILP was founded. After a big engineers' struggle there was a mass lockout in 1897-8; the Labour Representation Committee (forerunner of the Labour Party) was founded in 1900. During the Labour Unrest of 1910-14 the Labour Party played no role at all. That upsurge was halted by the war and re-emerged during it, largely through the shop stewards' movement, where again the Labour Party played no role.

At the height of the workers' offensive in 1919 the Labour Party had no role other than to carp at the workers' forward march. After its defeat, epitomised most dramatically by Black Friday (15 April 1921) when the Triple Alliance left the striking miners in the lurch, the Labour Party made big gains in the general election of 1922. After the engineers' fight and subsequent lockout of that same year, the Labour Party gained even more, forming the first Labour government in 1924.

After the defeat of the General Strike in 1926 the Labour

Party made sweeping gains in the local elections of 1927, and the Tories lost every by-election till the general election of 1929, when Labour took office for the second occasion, this time as the biggest party in parliament.

Political struggle and economic struggle are qualitatively different, although together they make a unity. As a force for leading the working class in a challenge to the capitalist state the Labour Party is totally bankrupt.

The trade unions cannot undertake this task alone either. The nature of trade unionism, reflecting the unevenness that riddles the working class and the sectionalism that rends it, makes the development of a specialised, conservative, bureaucratic leadership inevitable. While objectively rank-and-file workers have a common interest in opposing and overthrowing the system (whether they are aware of it or not!), union bureaucrats — reformist, centrist or verbally revolutionary — have a common group interest in confining workers' struggle within the system. Mass working-class struggle can knock the bureaucrats sideways, but it cannot turn them into revolutionaries — as it can the rank and file. The bureaucrats will continue to be a brake on the movement till a successful revolution.

As workers' struggle is expressed through their trade unions, therefore, it is not possible for them to break through the bounds of the capitalist system without the leadership of a revolutionary party which, active inside the unions, maximises their fundamental strengths and at the same time overcomes their deficiencies.

Lenin, in describing the symptoms of a revolutionary situation, pointed to the following:

> . . . When it is impossible for the ruling classes to maintain their rule without any change; when there is a crisis, in one form or another, among the 'upper classes', a crisis in the policy of the ruling class, leading to a fissure through which the discontent and indignation of the oppressed classes burst forth. For a revolution to take place, it is not usually sufficient for the 'lower classes not to want' to live in the old way; it is also necessary that 'the upper classes should be unable' to live in the old way.[1]

With the working class seething throughout the year, and the arms of repression liable to fail the state, these conditions existed in Britain in 1919. But the picture was incomplete. The situation was as revolutionary as it could be without the existence of a revolutionary party; it could more accurately be defined as a semi-revolutionary situation. Had there been a revolutionary party leading the working class, the split between Lloyd George and Churchill would have been sharpened considerably, and the vacillation between using force and persuasion would have polarised into an actual split in the ruling class itself. This a consistently revolutionary party could have exploited in order to destroy the bourgeois state. But that party was missing.

Introduction
1.   **Hansard**, 25 February 1919.

Chapter 1: The State Totters
1.   G W Reynolds and A Judge, **The Night the Police went on Strike** (London 1968) page 4.
2.   A Rothstein, **The Soldiers' Strikes of 1919** (London 1980) pages 37-9.
3.   Rothstein, pages 44-5.
4.   Rothstein, page 42.
5.   Rothstein, pages 42-64.
6.   Public Records Office (PRO), CAB 23/9, War Cabinet (WC) 514, 8 January 1919.
7.   Rothstein, pages 46-7.
8.   Rothstein, page 52.
9.   **Herald**, 11 January 1919.
10.   **Herald**, 11 January 1919.
11.   Rothstein, pages 69-75.
12.   Rothstein, page 70.
13.   Rothstein, pages 67-8, 80 and 85.
14.   **Hansard**, 29 May 1919.
15.   Davidson Papers, 10 January 1919, quoted in R K Middlemas, **The Clydesiders** (London 1965) page 89.
16.   **Hansard**, 14 May 1919.
17.   PRO, CAB 24/74 GT 6709, 27 January 1919.
18.   Rothstein, page 94.
19.   Rothstein, page 94.

20. PRO, CAB 23/9, WC 518, 22 January 1919.
21. Rothstein, page 95.
22. PRO, CAB 23/9, WC 532, 10 February 1919.
23. Rothstein, page 96.
24. Rothstein, page 97.
25. Quoted in Rothstein, page 100.
26. Rothstein, page 98.
27. PRO, CAB 23/9, WC 520, 28 January 1919.
28. PRO, CAB 23/9, WC 522, 30 January 1919.
29. PRO, CAB 23/9, WC 527, 5 February 1919.
30. PRO, CAB 23/9, WC 527, 5 February 1919.
31. PRO, CAB 24/73, GT 6654, 13 January 1919.
32. Rothstein, page 35.
33. Rothstein, page 10.
34. Quoted in D Gluckstein, **The Western Soviets** (London 1985) page 63.

Chapter 2: The Police Strikes

1. Reynolds and Judge, page 20.
2. Reynolds and Judge, page 27.
3. Reynolds and Judge, page 39.
4. Reynolds and Judge, page 46.
5. Reynolds and Judge, page 5.
6. Reynolds and Judge, page 55.
7. Reynolds and Judge, page 4.
8. Reynolds and Judge, page 68.
9. Reynolds and Judge, page 5.
10. Reynolds and Judge, page 76.
11. **The Police and Prison Officers' Magazine**, volume 1, number 2, 2 January 1919.
12. Reynolds and Judge, page 93.
13. Reynolds and Judge, page 116.
14. **The Police and Prison Officers' Magazine**, volume 1, number 16, 11 June 1919.
15. Reynolds and Judge, page 134.
16. Fifty-first Annual Trades Union Congress, **Report**, 8-13 September 1919, page 235.

17.   Reynolds and Judge, pages 145 and 147.

Chapter 3: The Forty Hours Strike

1.   A Hutt, **The Post-War History of the British Working Class** (Wakefield 1972) page 22.

2.   PRO, CAB 23/9, WC 523, 31 January 1919.

3.   PRO, CAB 23/9, WC 534, 3 February 1919.

4.   PRO, CAB 23/9, WC 523, 31 January 1919.

5.   K Jeffery and P Hennessy, **States of Emergency** (London 1983) page 10.

6.   PRO, CAB 23/9, WC 521, 28 January 1919.

7.   Gluckstein, page 60.

8.   H A Clegg, **A History of the British Trade Unions since 1889**, volume 2 (Oxford 1985) page 570.

9.   Gluckstein, page 55.

10.   See Gluckstein, pages 66-78.

11.   Gluckstein, page 84.

12.   Gluckstein, page 84.

13.   D S Morton, **The Forty Hours Strike** (Glasgow, no date) page 3.

14.   I McLean, **The Legend of Red Clydeside** (Edinburgh 1983) page 115.

15.   W Gallacher, **Revolt on the Clyde** (London 1936) page 218.

16.   McLean, page 116.

17.   McLean, page 129.

18.   McLean, page 117.

19.   McLean, page 117.

20.   J Leopold, 'The Forty Hours Strike' in **We Shall Be All** (Glasgow 1978) page 43.

21.   McLean, page 118.

22.   Morton, page 7.

23.   McLean, pages 118-9.

24.   Middlemas, page 92.

25.   McLean, page 119.

26.   J T Murphy, **Preparing for Power** (London 1972) page 179.

27.   Leopold, page 38.

28.   Middlemas, page 91.

29.   Morton, page 7.

30. Gallacher, pages 220-1.
31. Gallacher, page 226.
32. PRO, CAB 24/74, GT 6720, 29 January 1919.
33. PRO, CAB 23/9, WC 523, 31 January 1919.
34. Morton, page 13.
35. Morton, page 6; Gallacher, page 22.
36. Morton, page 6.
37. McLean, page 122.
38. Gallacher, page 233.

Chapter 4: The Miners

1. R Page-Arnot, **The Miners** (London 1953) page 69.
2. Rothstein, page 8.
3. PRO, CAB 24/73, GT 6663, 14 January 1919.
4. PRO, CAB 24/73, GT 6687, 22 January 1919.
5. Clegg, page 267.
6. PRO, CAB 24/74, GT 6720, 29 January 1919.
7. **Hansard**, 24 February 1919.
8. Page-Arnot, pages 184-5.
9. TUC **Report** (1919), pages 259-260.
10. Page-Arnot, page 185.
11. PRO, CAB 23/9, WC 523, 31 January 1919.
12. Clegg, page 267.
13. PRO, CAB 23/9, WC 528, 6 February 1919.
14. PRO, CAB 23/9, WC 528, 6 February 1919.
15. PRO, CAB 23/9, WC 528, 6 February 1919.
16. **Hansard**, 29 May 1919.
17. PRO, CAB 23/9, WC 527, 5 February 1919.
18. McLean, page 137.
19. **Hansard**, 21 March 1919.
20. PRO, CAB 24/73, GT 6687, 22 January 1919.
21. PRO, CAB 23/9, WC 529, 7 February 1919.
22. PRO, CAB 23/9, WC 529, 7 February 1919.
23. PRO, CAB 23/9, WC 528, 6 February 1919.
24. PRO, CAB 23/9, WC 529, 7 February 1919.
25. Jeffery and Hennessy, page 23.
26. A Hatchett, 'The Role of the **Daily Herald** with particular reference

to Direct Action, 1919-21', MA thesis, Warwick University, page 39.

27.   S R Ward, 'Intelligence Surveillance of British Servicemen', in **The Historical Journal**, volume 61, number 1 (1973) page 179.

28.   **Hansard**, 11 February 1919.

29.   PRO, CAB 23/9, WC 546, 19 March 1919.

30.   PRO, CAB 23/9, WC 546, 19 March 1919.

31.   **Hansard**, 25 February 1919.

32.   PRO, CAB 23/10, WC 553, 3 April 1919.

33.   Clegg, page 281.

34.   Labour Party Conference, **Report**, 25-27 June 1919, pages 112-3.

35.   **Hansard**, 17 February 1919.

36.   PRO, CAB 24/74, GT 6901, 26 February 1919.

37.   Hatchett, page 35.

38.   TUC **Report** (1919) page 261.

39.   V I Lenin, **Collected Works** (Moscow) volume 26, page 170.

40.   Lenin, volume 19, page 327.

41.   TUC **Report** (1919) page 262.

42.   Hatchett, page 35.

43.   Hutt, page 18.

44.   Hutt, pages 18-19.

45.   **Hansard**, 20 March 1919.

46.   Page-Arnot, page 201.

47.   PRO, CAB 24/76, GT 6976, 10 March 1919.

48.   Murphy, page 181.

49.   PRO, CAB 24/77, GT 7070, 2 April 1919.

50.   PRO, CAB 24/77, GT 7070, 2 April 1919.

51.   **Daily Herald**, 3 April 1919. (The weekly **Herald** became the **Daily Herald** on 31 March 1919.)

52.   Hatchett, page 137.

53.   TUC, **Report** (1919) page 262.

54.   PRO, CAB 24/77, GT 7091, 7 April 1919.

55.   **Hansard**, 24 February 1919.

56.   Murphy, page 182.

57.   Hutt, page 20.

58.   Clegg, page 287.

59.   **Hansard**, 18 August 1919.

60.   E Eldon Barry, **Nationalisation in British Politics: The Historical Background** (London 1965) page 242.

61.   Eldon Barry, page 243.

62.   Eldon Barry, page 243.

Chapter 5: The Railway Strike
1.   Clegg, page 570.
2.   P S Bagwell, **The Railwaymen** (London 1963) page 377.
3.   Bagwell, pages 377-8.
4.   **Hansard**, 24 February 1919.
5.   PRO, CAB 23/9, WC 536, 25 February 1919.
6.   PRO, CAB 23/9, WC 547, 1 March 1919.
7.   PRO, CAB 23/9, WC 547, 1 March 1919.
8.   Bagwell, page 379.
9.   Bagwell, page 377.
10.   Bagwell, page 379.
11.   Clegg, page 267.
12.   Hatchett, page 46.
13.   Beatrice Webb, quoted in Bagwell, page 386.
14.   Bagwell, page 381.
15.   Bagwell, page 382.
16.   Hatchett, page 55.
17.   Hatchett, page 29.
18.   Bagwell, pages 400-1.
19.   Jeffery and Hennessy, page 14.
20.   Hutt, pages 25-6; Bagwell, page 383.
21.   Bagwell, page 384.
22.   Clegg, page 289.
23.   Jeffery and Hennessy, page 16.
24.   Bagwell, page 377.
25.   Bagwell, page 395.
26.   Hutt, page 26.
27.   B and S Webb, quoted in Hutt, page 22.
28.   Bagwell, page 397.
29.   Hutt, page 28.
30.   Hutt, pages 27-8.
31.   Hatchett, page 56.
32.   Bagwell, pages 399-400.
33.   Bagwell, page 396.
34.   Bagwell, page 400.

35.   Bagwell, page 198; Hatchett, page 56.
36.   Hutt, page 27.
37.   Bagwell, page 399.

Chapter 6: How the Government Handled the Crisis
1.   PRO, CAB 23/9, WC 523, 31 January 1919.
2.   PRO, CAB 23/9, WC 521, 28 January 1919.
3.   **Herald**, 1 February 1919.
4.   TUC, **Report** (1919) page 289.
5.   T Cliff and D Gluckstein, **Marxism and Trade Union Struggle: The General Strike of 1926** (London 1986) page 75.
6.   TUC, **Report** (1919) page 262.
7.   Hutt, page 21.
8.   PRO, CAB 23/9, WC 533, 14 February 1919.
9.   **Herald**, 1 February 1919.
10.   TUC, **Report** (1919) page 53.
11.   **Hansard**, 29 May 1919.
12.   TUC, **Report** (1919) page 144.
13.   **Hansard**, 24 February 1919.
14.   PRO, CAB 23/9, WC 525, 4 February 1919.
15.   PRO, CAB 23/9, WC 522, 30 January 1919.
16.   Quoted in PRO, CAB 24/74, GT 6772, 5 February 1919.
17.   **Hansard**, 18 August 1919.

Chapter 7: The Trade Union Leaders
1.   Cliff and Gluckstein, page 26.
2.   Labour Party Conference, **Report** (1919) pages 119-120.
3.   Murphy, page 213.
4.   **Daily Herald**, 14 May 1919, quoted in Hatchett, page 38.
5.   TUC, **Report** (1919) pages 373-4.
6.   Cliff and Gluckstein, page 29.
7.   A Bevan, **In Place of Fear** (London 1952) pages 20-1.
8.   **Hansard**, 24 February 1919.
9.   **Hansard**, 11 February 1919.
10.   **Hansard**, 13 February 1919.

11.   **Hansard**, 13 February 1919.
12.   **Hansard**, 13 February 1919.
13.   **Hansard**, 24 February 1919.
14.   **Hansard**, 11 February 1919.

Chapter 8: Get Them Drunk!
1.   PRO, CAB 23/10, WC 583, 23 June 1919.
2.   PRO, CAB 23/9, WC 519, 24 January 1919.
3.   PRO, CAB 23/9, WC 544, 13 March 1919.
4.   PRO, CAB 23/9, WC 570, 22 May 1919.
5.   PRO, CAB 23/10, WC 573, 29 May 1919.
6.   PRO, CAB 24/76, GT 6976, 10 March 1919.
7.   PRO, CAB 24/81, GT 7417, 4 June 1919.

Chapter 9: Afterglow
1.   PRO, CAB 23/10, WC 584, 24 June 1919.
2.   TUC, **Report** (1919) page 220.
3.   TUC, **Report** (1919) pages 297-8.
4.   PRO, CAB 24/78, GT 7147, 23 April 1919.
5.   TUC, **Report** (1919) pages 218 and 231.

Chapter 10: Conclusion
1.   Lenin, volume 21, pages 213-4.

OTHER PUBLICATIONS

Bailing out the System
Reformist socialism in Western Europe 1944-1985
by Ian Birchall

In 1945 an astute Tory politician told the House of Commons: 'If you do not give the people reform, they are going to give you revolution.' In the years since then, reformism has again and again saved the capitalist system from disaster, defusing working-class struggle whenever it threatened to bring radical change. This book shows how.
£5.95 | US$12.00

Marxism and Trade Union Struggle: The General Strike of 1926
by Tony Cliff and Donny Gluckstein

The 1926 general strike put the political ideas of the day to the ultimate test of practice. In the light cast by the solidarity of millions of workers, the treachery of the trade union leaders gave a clear-cut shadow and the weaknesses of Community Party strategy were clearly outlined. This book uses an account of the strike to re-examine key questions for socialists today.
£6.25 | US$12.50

The Great Strike
The miners' strike of 1984-5
by Alex Callinicos and Mike Simons

The miners' strike of 1984-5 was a struggle of epic proportions. The Tory government mobilised all the forces of the state to crush the miners' union; villages were invaded and occupied by paramilitary police; the welfare state

was used to starve miners back to work. This is the story of the longest major strike in the history of the British working-class movement.
£3.95 | US$6.50

The revolutionary road to Socialism
by Alex Callinicos

Here is the case for revolutionary socialism, taking up the questions of why capitalism is in crisis worldwide, how the Labour Party and other reformist parties have failed, and what went wrong in Russia after the revolution of 1917.
£1.95 | US$3.00

The Western Soviets
Workers' Councils versus Parliament 1915-1920
by Donny Gluckstein

The workers' council movements of Italy, Germany, Britain and Russia proposed an alternative mass democracy to the parliamentary channels that failed in 1914, allowing the bloodbath of the First World War, and are failing now in a world of mass unemployment and economic crisis. This book examines an alternative now more urgently needed than ever.
£5.95 | US$11.00

'An Agitator of the worst type'
A portrait of miners' leader A J Cook
by Paul Foot

A J Cook was elected to lead the miners' union in 1924, the mid-point of a great period of confrontation between workers and employers that shook Britain. He led the miners through the 1926 general strike and the lock-out that followed.
95p | US$2.00

The Labour Party: Myth and Reality
by Duncan Hallas

Before the 1974 election victory, the Labour Party promised a 'massive and irreversible shift in the distribution of both wealth and power in favour of working people and their families.' It never happened. Under the 1974-9 Labour government unemployment rose by a million, prices doubled, health and education spending was cut drastically. This pamphlet explains why.

85p | US$1.50

These and many more publications are available from bookshops and local branches of the socialist organisations listed at the front of this book, or by post from:

- **Bookmarks**, 265 Seven Sisters Road, Finsbury Park, London N4 2DE, England.
- **Bookmarks**, PO Box 16085, Chicago, Illinois 60616, USA.
- **Bookmarks**, GPO Box 1473N, Melbourne 3001, Australia.

Bookmarks bookshop in London also runs a large socialist mail order service. We have stocks of books and pamphlets from many publishers on socialism, internationalism, trade union struggle, women's issues, economics, the Marxist classics, working-class history and much, much more. We're willing to send books anywhere in the world. Write for our latest booklists to:

BOOKMARKS, 265 Seven Sisters Road, Finsbury Park, London N4 2DE, England.